The Hormone P[uzzle]

Solving Infertility

INCLUDES
The
Complete
Hormone Puzzle
Cookbook

Along with over 100 additional recipes and even holiday recipes and a complete fertility meal plan.

They call m[e]
C♥ACH
Kela

Coach Kela Smith

WORKBOOK

© 2019 Coach Kela Smith

Cover by Daniel McCutcheon

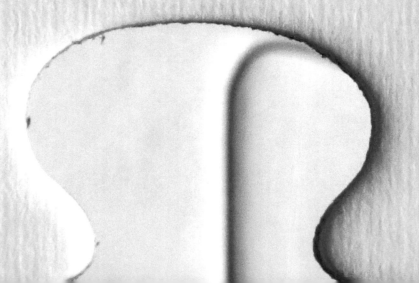

Hi,

I'm coach Kela Smith and I am a holistic health and wellness coach with over 20 years of experience in health education, fitness instruction and wellness coaching for women struggling with infertility and hormone imbalance and people struggling to lose weight. Working with women to help them achieve their dream of becoming a mom is truly my passion and the reason I was put on this earth!

Thank you for purchasing The Hormone Puzzle Method - Solving Infertility. This program will help you access your starting point, recommend simple action steps you can start taking today so you can step into empowered action and develop new habits that will put your body into the optimal state for conception so you can get pregnant naturally in 90 days or less. It's called the Puzzle method because we will talk about Proper Nutrition, Understanding Supplements, Zapping stress, Zzzzzz's (sleep), Love and encouragement and Exercise/movement. All the pieces you need to put together your hormone puzzle and create a healthy baby naturally.

You are probably wondering what my qualifications are - I hold 2 professional certifications through the Health Coach Institute in health and life coaching, HCI is an accredited school through the ICF (International Coaching Federation) and I am a certified personal trainer through ACE (American Council on Exercise). In addition, I hold 2 master's certifications in transformational coaching methods through Health Coach Institute.

Throughout my years of experience, I have worked with major corporations all over the country and was responsible for educating and training retail stores in fitness, nutrition, and wellness. I have also been a featured speaker and educator on nutrition, fertility, and lifestyle medicine throughout Nashville and the US. I am also the author of, *The Hormone Puzzle Cookbook, a cookbook for decoding your hormones and getting pregnant naturally.* Although I love speaking and educating, my main focus and passion is helping women and families realize their dream of becoming a mom and having the family they have so longed for.

My goal for this book is to educate, support and empower everyone I work with! I will provide all the encouragement and steps you need to create a healthy pregnancy and have a healthy baby.

I am determined to help women realize their own potential and put their bodies into the optimal state for conception in a way that is easy and fun. I take a lifestyle, holistic approach to wellness and the steps in this book help you to correlate your mind with your body and are a systematic approach to getting pregnant meaning we will work on the entire body and put it into symmetry, so it does what it was designed it to do.

Even if you have had years of "unexplained infertility", tried **EVERYTHING**, done fertility treatments and/or taken fertility drugs. I want you to go into this program with an open mind and heart. This time it can and will be different. If you trust yourself and this process,

Your dream of becoming a mom will be realized.

I got you! You can do this.

Visit www.hormonepuzzle.com to learn more about how working with a coach can change everything and watch my free masterclass, The Hormone Puzzle or enroll in my online program with the same name.

coach**kela**

www.**kelahealthcoach**.com

I am so happy you decided to purchase this book. I wrote this book with the purpose of helping you throughout your journey. The book is the most comprehensive "action-book" when it comes to getting pregnant and breaking the code in YOUR hormone puzzle. It has changed the lives of thousands of women all over the world and I can't wait for it to change yours.

This book will work perfectly if you go through it and has all the information you need to change your life, but it's good to know that the book is also **compatible** with The Hormone Puzzle Online Coaching program - www.hormonepuzzle.com

Many women choose to use the book in combination with the online program as well.

Through the online program, you'll have access to me and other women who have embarked on the same journey as you are about to start. If you need more personal support & guidance, I definitely recommend visiting www.hormonepuzzle.com and enroll in the online program.

Whichever way you choose is perfect for you in your journey. I got you. I am here.

Let's do this.

Join my Free Facebook Community

I highly recommend you also join my online Facebook community. In this group are women just like you, struggling with the same things as you. Use this group as added support, accountability or a place to just have fun. I am also moderating the group regularly and would love to hear from you. What are your celebrations, your fears, your triumphs and tribulations? I want to hear it all so please join us for this movement.

Join the group at The Hormone Puzzle - Decoding hormones and fighting infertility naturally.

Love and health,

Coach Kela

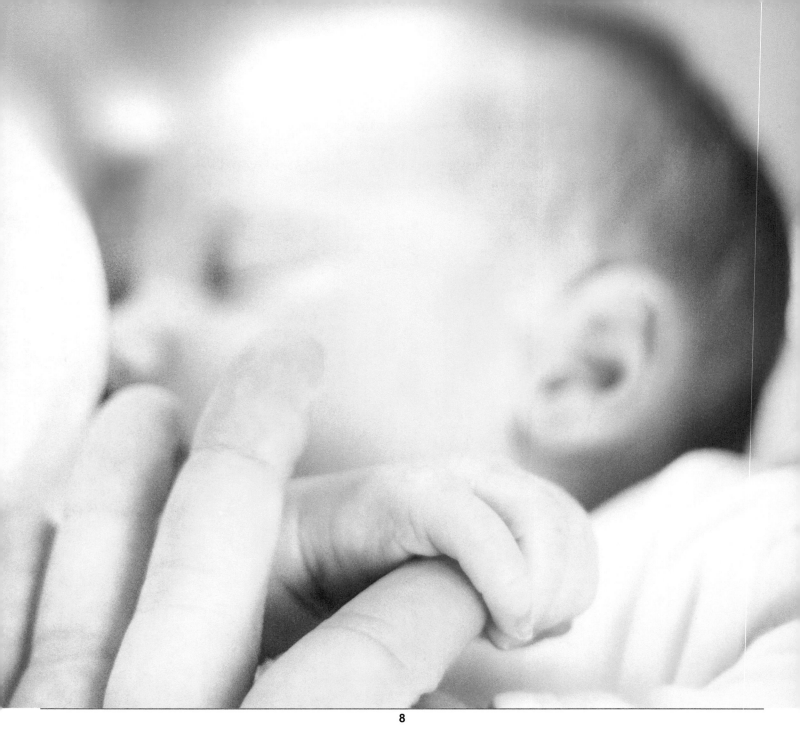

Table of Contents

Part 1

Part 2 – *Recipes*

I dedicate this book to my husband, Justin and 2 boys, Klayton and Koleton. For giving me the family I thought I would never have, for believing in me when sometimes I didn't believe in myself, for trusting me and allowing me to jump head first into a new realm of my career at 40 years old and for always trusting me to make the right decisions when it comes to my business and our future.

I love you all so much and I could never repay you for the life you have given me. My hope for this book is that it encourages another woman to go for her dreams the way I did and to begin to live the life she always knew she would.

"She thought she could, so she did. She flew and continues to fly"!

Part 1

Chapter 1

My Journey

To explain a little more about how I got here, I have to take you back to the beginning when I was growing up in Memphis, TN. My mother was a fitness fanatic. From a very young age, I would watch her go to exercise classes wearing her spandex leggings, leg warmers and bright colored headband (*it was the eighties, ya know*) and I knew I wanted to be just like her. From the moment she took me into a gym, I was hooked.

I loved all the fit people, the way it smelled, the familiarity that it brought me. Week after week and month after month I would go with her. Being such an impressionable kid, this was all it took for me to fall in love. As I got older, instead of just tagging along, I began to participate in some of the exercise programs from aerobics classes to weight lifting. It was not only a way for my mother and I to bond but it made me feel amazing.

I loved the feeling of getting nice and sweaty and feeling every muscle I had burn. It was my escape, it was my release, it was my zen place. My happy place.

Around the time I began actively participating in gym activities, I began experimenting in the kitchen. I knew that exercise was only half of the equation, but I didn't know exactly how nutrition played into things. Remember this was the eighties so the low-fat era was in full swing and I jumped on the bandwagon. Thinking lean cuisine and diet coke was good for me I was "eating healthy" and feeling great. As I continued this way for many years and into college, I thought I was doing it all right. I thought I was so healthy.

Little did I know that what I thought was healthy, wasn't healthy at all. A few more years of this and while attending Middle Tennessee State University for college and taking my first nutrition class, I knew that what I was eating wasn't as healthy as I thought, and it was time to make a change.

Around this time is when I decided to dive deeper into my love of fitness and become a certified personal trainer. I researched and decided to go for the ACE (American Council of Exercise) personal training certification. I realized my dream in early 2000 and was now a certified personal trainer.

It was while I was working as a PT that I began to really study and love nutrition. I was becoming a self-proclaimed nutrition nerd and wanted to learn everything I could about nutrition and how food affected the body. After college, I decided to take a job in the running industry as a wellness educator and merchandising rep. I was traveling to major cities and educating staff on how to sell our products, from nutrition products, running shoes, apparel, and fitness gadgets, I was in my dream job (or so I thought).

Throughout the 10 years of working for different companies in the wellness industry, there was still this nagging inside of me to dive back into a career more centered around nutrition. My inner nutrition nerd was aching to rear her head again and who was I to stop her.

It was around this time that I met my husband.

I had always wanted a family and knew from the night I met him that we would be together forever (*little did he know this*). Within a few months, we were professing our love for one another (*the first time this happened was at a Mindy McCreedy concert*) and planning our future.

We both knew we wanted a family, I probably wanted it more than him, but it didn't take long for us both to get on the same page. Once we got married, we started trying to get pregnant immediately, and like many couples thought it would be so easy. You hear your entire life to be careful or you might get pregnant which is what I did, and it worked but now that I wanted to get pregnant and was actively trying, I couldn't.

After about a year of trying naturally, we decided to seek out help. Our first stop was our doctor. She ran a few tests and told us what most doctors are trained to say, "I don't know why you aren't getting pregnant".

All our tests were normal and there was no valid reason why we couldn't get pregnant, so our prescription was to keep trying. Fast forward a few more months and a few more, "we got to do it now" conversations and still nothing.

This is when it became SO frustrating.

We were doing all the right things (so we thought), we were doing everything our doctor recommended. I was even taking fertility drugs, and NOTHING was working. After a few more months of this, we were encouraged to try a local fertility center.

I made an appointment immediately thinking, this is it.

They are going to help us once and for all.

They are the professionals.

They know what they are doing.

They will fix me.

What I wasn't prepared for, and what they suggested was IUI. I definitely didn't want to talk about IVF which I knew would be their next suggestion.

We had done the fertility drugs, we had done a few invasive procedures, I knew I didn't want to go any further with the traditional route. *I knew there had to be a better way.*

That is when it hit me. I had an epiphany. I had worked and studied in the nutrition and fitness industry my entire life. *I had the info inside of me.* I knew how to use food as medicine. Now was the time to take everything I knew about nutrition and holistic living and use it to get me pregnant.

This is when I became very intentional with what I was eating.

I was only going to eat the foods that were going to work with my body and not against it. I was going to clean up my diet in order to put my body into the optimal state for conception. I was going to eat delicious nutritious foods that were meant to increase fertility naturally and that is exactly what I did.

After about 6 months of eating intentionally and making some lifestyle changes, I became pregnant naturally.

OMG, we did it, I couldn't believe it. All my hard work had finally paid off. I was finally pregnant and was going to be a mommy. I cried! Even with an unexplained infertility diagnosis, even with years of trying, even with failed fertility drug rounds and betrayed invasive procedures, I was pregnant, at last, and I couldn't have been happier.

Fast forward 2 years and we decided we wanted to try again. The good news here is once I figured out what foods worked with my body and how to put my body into the optimal state for conception, I was able to get pregnant a second time fairly easily. I had done it. Not once but twice.

I had two beautiful baby boys and I couldn't have been happier or more fulfilled.

About a year after my second was born, I was still working in the fitness industry in a sales role I started doing some soul searching The more I read and saw friends and family members struggling with infertility, the more I decided something had to be done and I was the person that was put on this earth to do it.

I had to take action and help my sisters the way I so wished someone would have helped me. Through my research, I discovered The Health Coach Institute and their certifications. I could actually use everything I have learned through my own fertility research and turn it into a career.

This was a life-changing point in my life.

I knew what I had gone through was SO hard but now I had the answers. Now I had the knowledge on how to reverse infertility. I had the proof on myself. How could I not share this with the world? *So that is exactly what I am doing.*

I immediately enrolled in Health Coach Institute in their holistic health and life coaching certification program. Once I completed that I knew I wanted even more. I was becoming a sponge for all this nutrition knowledge and learning how to use food as medicine and how to make habit changes that would change my life and the lives of so many women. After completing 2 more certifications in transformational coaching methods and starting my holistic health and wellness practice focusing on women struggling to get pregnant and hormone imbalance, I am now working in my life's purpose and helping women all over the world become pregnant.

If I had to draw my ideal life, I couldn't have dreamed it would be this amazing and that is what I want for you.

Through this book and my work as a coach, I want to empower women that there is a different way, that this time it will work, that this time you can have the family and the life of your dreams. It's all within your reach.

The only request I have for you is to go into this new journey with an open heart and an open mind.

Even if you have tried **EVERYTHING**, even if you have tried all the traditional methods, fertility drugs, IUI, IVF, even if you think you have tried everything, I want you to know that this time can be different, this can be the turning point in your life.

The thing that changes everything. To get the most out of this book and program you must do the action steps. Information without empowered action is useless. Doing the action steps will be the difference between getting pregnant and just taking one more course or reading one more book that doesn't change your life. Now let's jump in and make your dreams a reality!

Congratulations mama! It's your time to finally decode your hormone puzzle and get pregnant naturally, once and for all

Love and Health, Coach Kela

Client Testimonial   - **Katie and Michael S.**

When I started working with this couple, they had been trying to conceive for about 4 years. Katie had some scarring on her fallopian tubes and the doctors were telling her she would probably never get pregnant.

This couple was DEVASTATED by this news.

Then they came across one of my videos on Facebook talking about how I have helped women all over the world overcome their infertility diagnosis and get pregnant naturally.

They decided to give me a call because they were tired of nothing working and they knew deep down there had to be a better way.

Once we started working together, this couple really put in the work. They got super intentional about what they were eating, and with my help, Katie was able to reduce inflammation in her body which allowed her blocked fallopian tubes to become unblocked. We also worked on Michael and getting his diet optimized for quality sperm and guess what…

SHE IS PREGNANT! After years of trying to conceive.

They couldn't believe it and couldn't be happier.

Chapter 2

Foundation Puzzle Piece - Week 1 of your Journey

** This chapter is compatible with **Week 1** of The Hormone Puzzle Online Coaching program. **

(www.hormonepuzzle.com)

In this chapter, we will be laying some foundational groundwork. First, we are going to be talking about where you are starting. Whether you work with me in a 1-1 program or taking one of my online classes, I always want to start with knowing where you are.

Please fill out the form at the end of this chapter.

This form will show you where you are, what you are currently doing, allow you to get really clear on your goals (I know you want a baby but what are small goals that will get you there), and help you to get really honest with yourself. Once you know where you are starting and you have a clear set action plan in place, it will make it much easier to reach these goals and surpass them.

We will be talking about determining your big MOFA (motivating factor). anchoring your MOFA and clearing your physical and emotional clutter from your environment to make room for this new way of being and this new life. It's hard to bring in something new if you don't get rid of something old.

Kind of like when you want a new couch. Unless you move out the old couch, there is no room in your living room. It's the same way when you want to bring home a baby.

Unless you are free of your physical and emotional clutter, there is no room for that baby. At the end of each chapter. you will have very specific action steps. **Please do these.**

This is what will be the difference between reaching your goal of creating a healthy baby or not. It's not just important to get the information but to actually apply it to your life and your situation so you can hit your goals of creating this baby.

"Information without empowered action is useless."

Action is what moves you forward. Action is what promotes habit change.

Your first step in this journey is to get in the mindset of thinking about what is going well.

Henry Ford said whether you think you can, or you think you can't, you are right.

The reason we start this way is that most of us are so used to focusing on what's not going well. What we are doing wrong, which must feel de-motivating. On the other hand, when we focus on what IS going well, we feel motivated and inspired to keep making progress.

So, I know that you have just started this book and we just began working together but I'm curious to start with something in your life that is going well with your health, your body, your family or something that you are proud of yourself for dong in the last 7 days.

Now write that down. Write it down somewhere that you can look at it often and remember it. I suggest getting a pretty journal that you can use throughout this program and during your pregnancy or using this book.

I have created a blank space for you to record your thoughts, feelings, emotions, action steps or anything that will help you through this journey. This workbook is your complete guide to decoding your hormones and getting pregnant naturally.

Starting each chapter with what is going well will help you start this course on a positive foot. This is a kind of currency that will motivate us to follow through even more. Like a self-acknowledgment. And it doesn't matter how small the acknowledgment is. Acknowledgment is a kind of fuel, it motivates us. It gives us energy. This is not about evaluating how well we did something. Or what we could have done better. It's not a test. All we are doing is recognizing ourselves for doing the best we can with what we have and then just whatever little effort we were able to do.

Congratulations!

Whatever you wrote down is perfect!

Feel how amazing it feels to acknowledge yourself in that way. We will start every chapter in this way. Can you feel how that shifts the energy of where you are coming from? This is key because this is the extra energy that we feel in surplus that allows us to make better decisions about our health and our body. On the other hand, when we are focused on what is not going well, we start to feel crappy and that tells our body not to make a baby because it is under stress.

I hope that makes sense to you.

Now we are going to do an exercise. I call this exercise the I AM exercise. This exercise will help to rewire your brain into a more positive mindset. The more you can tell your brain – You are something, the more that is what it hears and that is more the experience you will begin to have and that is who you will become. Our brains are like a big computer, we must program it to be what we want it to be.

Now we are going to talk about the desired state goal setting. What specific, measurable outcome do you want in the next 8 weeks and why? There are the 5 criteria for your SMART goals-

A well-formed outcome or goal is:

- o Stated in the positive (says what you want, not what you don't want).

- o Maintained and initiated by self (we don't need to rely on someone else changing).

- o Achievable within the time frame given.

- o Relevant to me and has a specific sensory-based description – so we know how it feels or looks. It would be easy to measure, or we have a description that would tell us when we have it.

- o Timely with an appropriate chunk size – biggest chunk to be worthwhile yet small enough to feel attainable.

When goal-setting, think of these as instructions to the universe, we want them to be specific, measurable, and achievable. Don't worry if you don't know what that means, I'm going to help you figure out what those are.

So, let's just start with an open brainstorm? What are some outcomes, maybe two or three outcomes that you'd like to have happen over the next 8 weeks? Like if you get that, you'd feel like, "This was the best investment ever."

Be as specific as possible –

You want to get pregnant and have a baby. You want to prepare your body to become pregnant, you want your fertility treatments to work better. This is just to get the WHAT. In a moment we will talk about the WHY and HOW. Asking these types of questions to yourself will help your body release anything it is holding that is blocking you from becoming pregnant.

1.   The Big Motivating Factor

(Affectionately known as The Big MOFA)

Once you know the **WHAT**, we need to know **WHY** you want it. Ask yourself these questions about your what- Example you want to get pregnant and have a healthy baby-

"What will having that do for you?" "What is important about that" "Who will be affected if you get this outcome" What will change in your life? What things will open up that wouldn't before?

Once you land on what is really important about this then you will know what is driving you to change or make the changes now that you haven't been willing to make in the past to reach this goal.

On a scale of 1-10, how important is this? If you aren't at least an 8, it's not a weighty enough. In that case, keep exploring until you find a valuable enough reason that you are making a commitment to follow through in ways you never have before.

2.   Anchoring the WHY or The Big Motivating Factor

An "anchor" is something physical in your environment that will remind you WHY you are doing this. It could be the screen saver of your computer, your wedding ring as a vow to yourself, or sticky notes around the house (which is my favorite anchors).

Choose an anchor for each of the 5 senses. Examples are:

- o   A picture of yourself or your family

- o   Your favorite perfume or a smell that you love.

- o   An object in your environment that has meaning or reminds you of something you love.

- o   or it can even be something on your own body (i.e. a knuckle, the forearm or the solar plexus)

I had a client once who chose her elbow as her anchor because she said anytime she looked in the mirror and her elbows looked "fat" to her she knew she had fallen off track. You can literally pick anything to anchor why you are doing this.

Here's how we will create anchors together –

A lot of the progress is happening outside of this book and my program, and unfortunately, I won't be there every moment when you're making choices. These anchors will be like your accountability buddy in between our sessions. Little reminders to make conscious choices rather than defaulting to old behaviors.

Let's create some anchors now. These are things in your physical environment that will remind you of why you're doing this. It could be a screensaver on your computer with an inspiring message, it could be a ring you wear, or notes around the house, one of your jewelry pieces, a song you sing. These anchors will pair up with your MOFA's. So, what will happen is when you see it or hear it, it will remind you of your Big Motivating Factors.

And it can do two things. It can be a pattern interrupt, stop you like a record scratch when you're tempted to make a choice which may not be in alignment with your outcomes here, or it can just give you that influx of energy of like, "Oh ya! I want to do X for myself!" And give you that creative spark that you kind of had at the beginning when you were talking about what's going well. It can help prevent us from making incongruent choices for ourselves, and it can also give us that little infusion of life like

'Oh Yeah. I'm excited about making this a good choice for myself at this moment!'

Does that make sense?

Now that you have your big MOFA or motivating factor and you have your anchors I want to talk about clearing any physical or emotional clutter from your environment.

Clear the Clutter Exercise

Have you started something in the past and not finished it? Have you had an important goal and were gung-ho about it but then a few weeks in you fell off the wagon? You just gave up. Things got really hard, so you abandoned your dreams for the easy route? Most people have made goals in the past and not achieved them, and part of it is because they haven't systematically or structurally changed anything in their life to make way for the new thing.

We must clear out the old furniture before we can bring in the new.

"Is there any clutter in your schedule or environment that needs clearing before you can move forward?"

Let's brainstorm for 2-3 minutes and make a list of all the things which could possibly get in the way of you committing to yourself over the next 8 weeks.

Which of these are **within your control**? Put a star next to the things that are within your control. Which of these needs clearing so that you have the conditions for success from the beginning?

Action Steps –

I like to give action steps after each week. As I explained in the beginning. Knowledge without empowered action is useless. Action is what will be the needle mover and will be the difference between this program working or not. Take 1-2 empowered action steps this week before you move on to Chapter 2.

Here are some examples of actions you can take to move you forward. Pick 1-2 of these or choose your own. Remember this is your journey so whatever you choose is perfect for you.

1. Clear the clutter and set the conditions for success.

   You will focus on the current roadblocks that are in your control and take action towards clearing them out. Maybe this is something to do with setting sacred appointments with yourself or cleaning your closet, pantry or mind.

2. Connect with your anchors.

   Make it mean something! Write down your vow statement in this book. Notice when you make choices that are not in alignment with this promise to yourself. No need to judge it, approach it compassionately and consciously. Every time you see, touch, hear your anchor, it's a moment of truth:

   "Am I making the best choice for myself at this moment?"

   If the answer is no, then make a different choice.

3. The AWARENESS Action – pick ONE action around physical awareness.

   I want you to get connected to your body. This week I want you to experiment with your breakfast. Eat your typical breakfast and note how you feel afterward. Did you have energy or not, did you have an upset tummy or were you hungry an hour later? Really get curious about your breakfast and how it is serving you and moving you toward your goals of getting pregnant.

I like to end each chapter with you writing down what your aha's and appreciations are about this chapter and about these new action steps. This will have you ending each chapter on a positive note and give you fuel to keep moving forward.

NOTES

NOTES

NOTES

NOTES

Week 1 Journal Page

Why do you want a baby?

_____

_____

_____

What will having that do for you?

_____

_____

_____

How will your life change when you become pregnant and have a baby?

_____

_____

_____

Imagine that you are already pregnant, how does it feel? What will you see, feel, hear, think?

_____

_____

_____

Where, when, and with whom do you want it with?

_____

_____

_____

What has your life been like up till now?

_____

_____

_____

What are your feelings around not being able to conceive up until this point?

_____

_____

_____

Who else in your life might be affected positively or negatively if you were to get pregnant?

_____

_____

_____

What, if anything might you have to let go of in order to allow yourself to get pregnant?

_____

_____

_____

Imagine yourself pregnant, what are the feelings you are feeling, what will others see, how will you be different when this is your reality?

_____

_____

_____

_____

_____

_____

_____

_____

_____

_____

_____

_____

_____

_____

_____

_____

_____

Daily Mantra –

I am,

Free Curious Certain Devine abundant Brave Adventurous Lucky Devoted Present Loved Patient Grateful Ready Wise Passionate Strong Centered Alive The creator of my reality Clear Experienced Powerful Unburdened Lit Gifted Vibrant Awakened Important Gentle Energetic Intuitive Increasing Beautiful Connected Expansive Kind Elated Enough Centered Grounded Fearless Hopeful Good Elated Strong Centered Protected Valuable Vulnerable Worthey Accepting Insightful Balanced Magic Honest Healthy Rested Graceful Grateful

Choose one of these I am statements or create your own. This is a powerful exercise that will re-wire your brain and have you moving forward with ease.

Intake Form

Disclaimer:

Fill this page out to show you where you are starting and use it as a reference to get really clear on your starting point. This will help you when moving forward.

1. How long have you been trying to have a baby or struggling with hormone imbalance?

_____
_____
_____

2. Are you struggling with first or secondary infertility?

_____
_____
_____

3. What have you done in the past to work on this condition (include both alternative and traditional modalities)?

_____
_____
_____

4. What has proven effective?

_____
_____
_____

5. What is your current diet like? Please be specific: list breakfast, lunch, dinner, and snacks, as well as the times you eat.

_____
_____
_____

6. Are you taking any supplements? Please list what you take and what its for.

_____

_____

_____

7. What is your desired outcome for reading this book or participating in this online program?

_____

_____

_____

8. What obstacles, challenges, and struggles do you come up with regarding diet/lifestyle?

_____

_____

_____

9. Have you seen a fertility specialist and what was their diagnosis OR have you been to a hormone specialist and what was the outcome?

_____

_____

_____

10. Are you committed to investing in yourself over the next 8 weeks to complete this book and this program and are you committed to doing the action steps?

_____

_____

_____

Clear Kitchen Clutter

Kitchen Area #1: Fridge & Freezer & Pantry:

a) Check expiration dates and toss expired products.

b) Clean out any trans fats and GMOs.

c) Wipe down and/or wash shelves.

d) Decide what 1-2 new foods you want to try this week and start to restock your pantry, freezer and fridge with those items.

Kitchen Area #2: Utensil Drawers:

a) Keep 1-2 the prettiest, most useful items and donate the rest (for example, instead of having 5 can openers, keep your best one and take the rest to Goodwill).

b) Go through your Tupperware and throw out or donate any miss-matched items.

c) Go through any dishes. Which ones are mismatched or broken? Donate or throw away anything that isn't serving you.

Kitchen Area #3: Cabinets:

a) Find at least 3 unused kitchen gadgets or items and take them to Goodwill.

b) Donate any processed food or food with very high sugar. This can be done in stages if you aren't comfortable doing it all at once.

c) Check the fridge, what is expired, what is left over that you won't eat, what is processed.

d) Freezer- same

Client Testimonial   - **Stephanie and Tom P.**

When I started working with this couple that had been doing fertility treatments for a while and nothing was working. The doctors kept telling them nothing was wrong, and they should keep trying.

Needless to say, they were FRUSTRATED and EXHAUSTED.

They decided they wanted to take their fertility into their own hands and so they called me.

After determining what they were currently doing we were able to make small adjustments to their nutrition, so we were intentionally eating for fertility, supplement where needed, we got her cycle back on track and a few other minor changes.

And guess what- STEPHANIE IS PREGNANT! After years of trying to conceive.

Needless to say, they couldn't be happier.

This could be you!

Chapter 3

Fertility Reset Puzzle Piece

** This chapter is compatible with **Week 2** of The Hormone Puzzle Online Coaching program. **

(www.hormonepuzzle.com).

Hey girlfriend, how did last week go? What went well for you?

I hope you were able to implement some of what you learned. I know in the beginning it can seem hard or like you aren't making much progress but remember,

Tons of things are happening under the surface.

So much is happening in your mind. So many subconscious things. I want to encourage you to trust the process and continue to move forward. No matter how small the changes you are making are. Continue doing 1 thing that moves you forward every day and I promise you will see results.

So, let's begin this chapter and week again with what is going well. This is not time to focus on what we are doing wrong, which will feel so de-motivating. On the other hand, when we focus on what IS going well, we feel motivated and inspired to keep making progress.

So, I am curious.

What went well this week?

Were you able to implement the action steps from last week?

Either way, ask yourself why or why not? Get really curious if you didn't follow through on your action steps or if the week didn't go as planned. How can you course-correct to make it go better next week? What are some specific actions you can take to set yourself up for inevitable success?

Write those down in your journal or in this book.

(Did you see this book also serves as your journal?)

Getting these thoughts out of your head and onto paper is so motivating and will be just what you need to keep moving forward.

This week we will be talking about how to reset our bodies by removing toxins, healing from within and setting ourselves up to create and sustain a healthy pregnancy and baby.

We will be discussing what foods you will need to eat and which activities you'll need to be doing in order to clean the slate and get your body in optimal health and state for conception.

So why do we do a reset?

I do this reset first with all my clients because this is the pathway to release toxins and excess bloat from your tissues, reset your digestive system and renew your baseline of wellbeing and start to put your body into that optimal state for conception.

You will learn how food affects the way you feel, how to attune to your body's unique needs and activate your natural healing potential.

Doing all of this before you start trying to get pregnant is essential if you want to start on the right foot. Sometimes you have toxic buildup, unknown food allergies or blocks that are preventing you from getting pregnant. Starting this program with a clean slate will make the difference between it working or not.

Your destiny is determined by the choices you make, Choose now, Choose well

- Anthony Robbins

The number one cause of infertility in this country is high blood sugar which leads to PCOS and is an ovulatory condition. Many women are accustomed to eating a diet high in sugar and processed foods which leads to toxic overload in the body.

During this reset, we will help your body start to release these toxins and start to heal from within, so we can set ourselves up for optimal health and baby-making. Sugar is also an inflammatory food and when your body is inflamed which is an emergency signal to the body that makes the immune system hyper-reactive over time and slows wound healing. This alarm in the body sends a signal that it's not a safe environment to reproduce. Sugar also raises cortisol which throws off our hormones, digestion, and sleep.

The other reason for doing a reset is because we take in toxins from all around us. From the food we eat that has pesticides and herbicides on it, to the water we drink, the air we breathe to household chemicals we use. These toxins are everywhere. Our body wants to protect us from these toxins, so it builds fat cells to go around our organs to protect us. During this time, it sends signals to the brain to stop all processes and this includes making a baby.

If you can release these toxins, then your body realizes it is safe and baby-making commences.

What should you expect during these next 28 days?

Are you ready to be completely challenged, stretched beyond comfort, and transform your body like never before? What if it meant you would finally optimize your body for fertility and you would get pregnant and once you had that baby and you knew what steps to take for optimal health, you could put your body into the best shape of your life.

Putting your body into the optimal state for conception and intentionally eating for fertility, means so much more than just "eating healthy" or taking fertility drugs or supplements. It requires a complete commitment to your health which requires you to change your relationship to food and your body, once and for all.

You can't just eat healthy or workout a bad diet, relying on this alone to transform your health and weight is just wishful thinking.

This reset is a pathway to release toxins and excess bloat from your tissues, reset your digestive system and renew your baseline for wellbeing so you get pregnant naturally. You will learn how food affects the way you feel, how to attune to your body's unique needs and activate your natural healing and baby-making power.

Maybe you have been settling for "pretty good" where your health and weight are concerned. It's easy to become normalized to being overweight, unhappy and unhealthy. Heck, the typical American is 20-30lbs overweight. It's the new normal.

Is that how you want to look and feel? Are you ok walking through life in a fog? Are you happy with your energy level and do you have enough energy for the things you love? It's time for new ideas, goals, and tools so you can get pregnant once and for all and be at optimal health and fertility.

You owe it to yourself and your potential family to really evaluate where you are now, and then decide where you want to be. This program requires dedication (especially the reset part) and discipline. What it doesn't require is starvation and deprivation. Yes, your grocery bill will be a little higher, yes you might have to cook at home some, however, your doctors' bills will be lower, and you will get pregnant like you so desire.

Let's get started with walking you through YOUR reset.

What should I expect...

4 easy to follow phases

Changing your eating habits will take some getting used to... here is a basic play- by-play of what you may experience.

1 PRE-RESET PREP (2 DAYS)
The Pre-Reset is about making the commitment, setting your intentions, shopping for reset friendly ingredients, and beginning to ease your body into the full reset, mentally, emotionally and physically.

2 RESET (7 DAYS)
During the reset you will follow the simple elimination diet plan and body practices. You will be aiming to cook your meals in advance and have plenty of ready-to- grab options at the ready to avoid making "hangry" selections!

3 RE-INTRODUCTION (5 DAYS)
In the Re-introduction phase, you will re-introduce foods back in to your diet one by one to identify food sensitivities and intolerances and create a maintenance diet that best serves your unique body.

4 MAKING HABITS LAST (14 DAYS)
Move into a clean eating plan with Coach Kela's guidance, accountability and support

week 1
During the first week, your body will be adjusting... it will be eliminating dietary triggers and sensitivities. You may/will feel tired and sluggish as your body is working really hard to start releasing toxins. Stay positive!

week 3
This is where you start to feel lighter, more energized and clear headed. You have officially habitualized this clean lifestyle and you won't give up any time soon. You will find knowing what to eat and has become second nature.

week 2
After working through the initial detox, you will start having more energy and sleeping more soundly. Your energy gets higher, caffeine, sugar, carb cravings etc. start to become a thing of the past.

week 4
You have lost a little weight (average up to 10lbs.). Most of my clients say they gained A LOT of energy, and felt very uplifted and ready to move into the next phase with these new learned health habits.

Ready, Set, Go!

1 PRE-RESET PREP (2 DAYS)

✓ Set your schedule: decide WHEN you will begin & put it on your calendar!

✓ Let's work to identify your goals + support network.

✓ Get rid of any "toxic temptations" in your home & work environment.

✓ Review the shopping list & supplies and then set time for shopping.

✓ Plan out time for prep, cooking and recording notes in your journal.

✓ Identify time for exercise, stretching and rest that your body may need.

So here is the big question...

What Do I eat?

Phase 2 -

 RESET (7 DAYS)

Simple, clean foods that are all organic (all meat from pasture raised, grass fed animals), easy to prepare and easy to digest... this protocol is designed to eliminate major foods that cause inflammation and digestive issues. You will see that there are plenty of foods to choose from! Focus on what you get to have, not what you don't!

Meat, Poultry, Fish
- 1 package chicken breasts
- 2 freshwater salmon filets
- 2 freshwater halibut filets
- 1 package tofu

Grains & Beans
- 1 box rice cereal
- 1 box quinoa
- 1 bag dried lentils
- 1 loaf of rice bread (Food for Life)

Non-Dairy Milk & Broths
- 1-gallon unsweetened vanilla almond milk
- 1 bottle unsweetened coconut water
- 1 (32 oz) no sodium added veggie broth
- 2 cans unsweetened full-fat coconut milk

Fruits
- 1 bag frozen cherries / blueberries
- 2 mangos
- 3 limes
- 1 container of blueberries
- 1 lemon
- 3 gala apples
- 2 peaches

Nuts & Seeds
- 1 bag raw almonds
- 1 bag of raw pumpkin seeds
- 1 bag raw sunflower seeds
- 1 bag unsweetened coconut
- 1 bag ground flax seed

Veggies
- 1 bag spinach
- 1 bunch of dino kale
- 2 scallions
- 2 medium leeks
- 1 parsnip
- 5 avocados
- 1 bag carrots
- 1 purple cabbage
- 1 zucchini
- 1 bag celery stalks
- 1 box mushrooms
- 1 bunch kale
- 1 red pepper
- 1 white onion
- 3 medium butternut squash
- 1 bag romaine lettuce leaves

Animal Sources

Chicken, Turkey, Cod, Halibut, Wild Salmon, Sole, Trout

Dried Beans

Adzuki, Black Beans, Garbanzo, Kidney, Lentils, Pinto, Split Peas, Mung Beans.

Nuts, Seeds, Oils

Raw Only: Do Not Cook
Hemp, Pumpkin, Flax, Sunflower, Sesame, Tahini, Almonds, Walnuts, Brazil Nuts, Pine Nuts, Pumpkin Butter, Walnuts, Pumpkin Oil, Sesame Seeds, Walnut Oil, Almonds, Flax Seeds, Hemp-seeds, Nut Butters, Olive Oil (extra-virgin cold-pressed), Coconut Oil (Virgin, unrefined)

Veggies

Mushrooms (all varieties), Olives, Parsnips, Beets, Radicchio, Rhubarb, Carrots, Squash, Zucchini, Rutabaga, Kale, Green Beans, Scallions, Spinach, Bok Choy, Cucumbers, Snap Peas, Fennel, Leeks, Sprouts, Lettuces, Broccoli, Celery, Purple Cabbage

Fruits

Nectarines, Peaches, Artichoke, Jicama, Cherries, Gala Apples, Watermelon, Pomegranate, Grapefruit, Cranberries, Pears, Raspberries, Apricots, Lemons, Mangos, Pears, Papaya, Pineapple, Avocado, Kiwi, Limes, Blackberries, Plums and Blueberries.

Grains

Amaranth, Buckwheat, Brown Rice, Cream of Rice, Rice Bread, Rice Crackers, Rice Milk, Rice Pasta, Millet, Mochi (no dried fruit – read labels) Tapioca, Teff.

Superfoods & Other

Spirulina, Sea Veggies, Adzuki Bean, Miso, Spices and Fresh Herbs.

Breakfast

+ *pick one* +
- ✓ touch down shake
- ✓ the fifty-yard line shake
- ✓ cream of rice cereal
- ✓ rice bread toast with nut butter and avocado

+ *pick one* +
- ✓ water
- ✓ decaf tea
- ✓ herbal tea
- ✓ teeccino
- ✓ green tea

Lunch

+ *pick one* +
- ✓ 1-2 cups of give me green salad
- ✓ 1-2 cups of rainbow salad
- ✓ 1-2 cups of veggie stir-fry with ¼ cup quinoa

+ *pick one* +
- ✓ 1 serving of chicken
- ✓ 1 serving of salmon
- ✓ 1 serving of tofu
- ✓ 1 serving of halibut

+ *pick one* +
- ✓ 1 to 2 TBSP olive oil dressing
- ✓ 1 to 2 TBSP red wine vinegar
- ✓ 1 to 2 TBSP avocado dressing

+ *pick one* +
- ✓ water
- ✓ decaf tea
- ✓ herbal tea
- ✓ teeccino
- ✓ green tea

Dinner

+ *pick one* +
- ✓ 1-2 cups of gentle lentil soup
- ✓ 1-2 cups of thai squash soup
- ✓ 1 to 2 fish tacos

+ *pick one* +
- ✓ ½ cup quinoa 1 cup broccoli
- ✓ 1 cup asparagus

+ *pick one* +
- ✓ 1-2 TBSP olive oil dressing
- ✓ 1-2 TBSP red wine vinegar
- ✓ ½ avocado

+ *pick one* +
- ✓ water
- ✓ decaf tea
- ✓ herbal tea
- ✓ teeccino
- ✓ green tea

Snack

+ *pick one (2x a Day)* +
- ✓ 1 gala apple
- ✓ 1 pear
- ✓ 1 white peach
- ✓ 1 cup watermelon
- ✓ 1 TBSP almond butter
- ✓ 1 TBSP cashew butter
- ✓ ¼ cup almonds
- ✓ ¼ cup walnuts

* *Special Instructions!* *

At breakfast and dinner, you are to drink the flax seed cocktail, warm lemon water and detox tea.

Key Points to Remember:

Q: What should I eat?

A: You can eat anything on the page labeled *what should I eat.* You can choose to eat from the pick two menu that I provided, or you can choose to make your own menu based on the approved foods list in the right-hand column, you can even mix it up and pick some from my list and some of your own creations. Whatever you choose is perfect for you. Have fun with your menu, experiment with new foods and flavors that you haven't tried before. If you don't know how to prepare something, look for a recipe in one of my cookbooks or look on the internet. There are SO many wonderful recipes, all you have to do is start creating.

Q: How do I get myself and my home ready for my program?

A: Decide WHEN you will begin and put it in your calendar AND post it proudly on your fridge! You will need to block some time in your schedule for shopping and prepping foods ahead of time, so you are not tempted to veer off the program due to a desperate "hangry" freak out episode. Get rid of any "toxic temptations" such as bread, anything with sugar, chips, beverages… basically, rid your home of any items on the "do not eat" list. If it's out of sight, it is out of mind.

Q: How important is planning ahead?

A: Planning is everything! You are much more likely to stick with the program if you have a clear plan of what to eat. I will help you create your own meal plan using the tools received upon program sign up. For a little while, eating at work or out at restaurants and social gatherings is going to be challenging. It is best to be equipped with your foods for success. A little advance planning is going to be your key to success.

Q: Do I really need to keep a journal?

A: Yes, some note-taking is advised as it helps us learn and determine when you are feeling preoccupied with food or get hit with a challenge to overcome a snack attack. Awareness gives us more range to make empowered choices that support our best health!

Q: Omg… do I really need to give up coffee!?!

A: We've been there…We know how much that cup of Joe is part of your daily life. The answer is yes, you really do have to give up all coffee, decaf included for the first 7 days. Coffee is very acidic and dehydrating, and caffeine severely taxes the detox organs, such as the liver and kidneys. Here's what I suggest you do to let go of coffee during your journey enjoy a: GREEN Smoothie, TECCINO (This is a super yummy coffee substitute), GREEN TEA or YERBA MATE: These are great substitutes - energizing and full of additional health benefits. (see how-to coffee guide resource at the end of this chapter).

Q: Do I really need to buy all organic food?

A: Yes. Non-organic produce contains pesticides, herbicides and icky stuff that overworks your liver and increases toxicity in the body. Organic foods are more nutritious, and you'll be satisfied with less food, so you feel light and energized after eating. Yes, organic foods do cost more, but you're worth it, especially during your reset and as you are preparing your body to create and sustain life.

Q: Can I exercise during the 28-day reset?

A: Yes, yep, absolutely… you better, you bet! Regular exercise is recommended but do pay attention to your body's signals to rest or conserve energy and choose activities accordingly. Choose a gentle or restorative exercise that provides a deep mind/body connection.

Q: What sort of symptoms/side effects can I expect during the reset?

A: In a well-designed program such as this one, you need not feel like crap, but you will likely experience some symptoms. After all, you are eliminating bad things from your body and detoxing! Symptoms may include: increased body odor, bad breath, fatigue, headaches, irritability, chilliness, dry lips and skin (dehydration!), constipation or increased mucus discharge. If you are experiencing strong, unpleasant symptoms, it may be an indication that your tissues are releasing toxins faster than your eliminating organs can excrete them. This will pass.

Q: Why am I craving sugar… help!

A: Your cravings are usually caused by one or a combination of three factors: detoxing, under-eating, and emotional imbalance. So, we need to determine together what may be happening. If it is your body detoxing, upping your alkalizing foods such as dark green leafy vegetables will help the feelings pass. If you are under-eating, we need to adjust so you are eating enough nutrient-dense foods. Sometimes cravings for sweet flavor are an indication we are yearning for more sweetness in our lives. Consider what you might really be needing? Love, approval, a hug, play, social time, solo time, a walk in nature, a massage, or perhaps you need to just put on some great music and dance!

Q: Hummmm, I've heard that reset programs can make you constipated, is that true?

A: Most people do not experience such side effects but to prevent constipation make sure you are drinking at least 2 liters of water a day and move your body! Do daily walking, jogging, yoga, stretching, especially twists. Constipation can make the belly feel very full. You may want to reduce food intake until your bowels empty. If you've tried the prevention techniques above, and you're still not going easily (at least once a day), here are some other options:

1. **Belly Massage:** Start with lying on your back with your knees up. Begin in the lower right area of your belly. Press deeply with your fingertips. Work clockwise along the soft area below your ribcage.
2. **Laxative Tea:** Drink one strong cup twice a day of Traditional Medicinal "Smooth Move" tea.
3. **Magnesium Citrate:** Magnesium Citrate promotes healthy bowel function. Take 2-3 capsules 2x/day until your bowels start moving again. Be mindful of your dosage.

Q: What things I can do to enhance the removal of toxins?

A: I'm glad you asked! There are several things you can practice or participate in that helps the body get rid of those nasty toxins.

1. **Saunas**: One of the ways the human body removes toxins and speeds up metabolism is through sweating! The importance of being well hydrated before and during a sweating treatment cannot be overemphasized. This means sipping water over a long period before, not just guzzling a bunch of water immediately before or during your sauna. To maximize health benefits, alternate between 10 minutes in a sauna, followed by a cold plunge or shower. *Be sure to consult your doctor before taking a sauna if you are pregnant or have a heart or kidney condition.

2. **Stretching, massage & exercise:** All of these provide you with important opportunities to love and pay attention to your body, relieve stress, improve circulation, and improve muscle and organ health. Easy stretching and exercising should be included daily. Massage treatments are excellent and a great reward for a job well done!

3. **Breathing techniques:** Doing some simple breathing exercises for five minutes once a day is a great practice. Your goal is simply to keep your attention on the breath cycle and observe. This is a basic form of meditation, a relaxation method, and a way to begin to harmonize body, mind, and spirit.

4. **Detox Tea:** Detox tea usually includes gentle cleansing herbs that promote healthy liver function such as burdock, dandelion, licorice root, fennel seed and nettles. You can find a caffeine-free Detox Tea at your local health food store. Add a sprinkle cayenne pepper to it for an added kick.

Check my Fullscript dispensary for my recommendation on my favorite detox tea and to order with my practitioner discount.

https://us.fullscript.com/welcome/coachkela

5. **Hot water bottle:** Hot water bottles aren't just for old-timers. it is one of the most useful all-purpose health care products you will ever use! It is designed to apply comfortable, soothing heat therapy easily and conveniently to any part of the body, for a variety of ailments. Use it on your abdomen to aid in digestion or apply to back to relax.

Q: How much water should I drink?

A: During this reset your body is working very hard to eliminate toxins, heal, and reset so making sure you are properly hydrated is key as well as making sure all the toxins your body is releasing are being flushed out.

You want to make sure you are drinking *.67 x your body weight in ounces per day.*

In the beginning, this may seem hard, but it is non-negotiable. If you currently aren't drinking this much water, you will want to start slow. Think of your body as a sponge. If you try to pour water on a dry sponge, what happens? It runs off the top. However, if you add it slowly then it will absorb.

Adding water 8-16oz per day until you reach your minimum amount is key.

If it is extremely hot where you live or if you are exercising a lot, you will need more.

Next, you'll find a guide I have made to help you with your water intake.

How Much Water to Drink?

- o Drink between 64 ounces and 0.67% of your body weight
- o For example, if your body weight is 150 pounds, then you need to drink anywhere between 64 ounces and 100 ounces (0.67% x 150) of water per day.

The amount of water you'll drink depends on:

- o The amount of water you were drinking before you began
- o Your level of activity (how much you sweat ;-))
- o How much caffeine or alcohol you drink daily (*Both caffeine and alcohol are dehydrating, so be sure you go "1- for-1"*)
- o The temperature where you live. Super-hot summers require more water.

You can tell that you're drinking enough water when:

- o Urine is on the light side. If the urine is dark and there's not much of it, then you're likely not drinking enough water.
- o Urine is abundant
- o You must empty your bladder about every two or three hours. If you're going constantly, you could be drinking too much water.

NOTE: When you first start to increase water consumption, you WILL be in the bathroom more often than you're used to, but that will only last a few days and then the body will adjust.

How to Drink Water When You Don't Like the Taste of Water:

- o Add slices of lemon, lime, cucumber or orange
- o Add mint leaves
- o Add your favorite flavor Emergency-C for sparkle and taste
- o Drink your favorite flavor herbal tea, iced or hot
- o Use a fabulous drinking glass or goblet!
- o Heat water and drink with lemon

- Drink 20 oz (*1-2 glasses*) of water first thing in the morning. You've been asleep for 6 to 10 hours, so it's time to hydrate! This can even replace morning coffee, as rehydrating the body and brain will lead to clearer thinking and better energy.

- Keep a lovely pitcher of filtered water in your fridge at home or near your workspace with the amount of water you want to drink. This makes it easy to remember to drink water and to track your intake.

- Drink an 8 oz of water before exercise. Sip water during exercise.

- Bottles, bottles everywhere! Keep glass bottles of water in your car, at the office, or around your work areas. If you can't access a filter for your water, then let drinking water stand at room temp for an hour or more. This reduces the amount of chlorine in drinking water, as the chlorine will evaporate.

- If you have digestive challenges, drink most of your water between meals.

- Add ConcenTrace Trace Minerals, Celtic Sea Salt or Green Powder to water to increase nutrient content and improve the pH of your body.

An easy way to get more water into your diet and eat some delicious foods is to add these 8 foods to your diet today.

1. **Strawberries-** These yummy little berries are comprised of 92% water. They are so delicious and versatile. You can eat them by themselves or add them to smoothies or toppings for oatmeal or desserts.

2. **Cantaloupe-** These delicious melons are 90% water and provide you with beta carotene, vitamin A, and vitamin C. They can be eaten by themselves, wrapped in prosciutto(antipasto) or as a topping on a salad.

3. **Celery-** At 95% water, this yummy veggie is rich in vitamins and minerals with a low glycemic index. You'll enjoy vitamins A, K, and C, plus minerals like potassium and folate when you eat celery. It's also low in sodium. Having a low glycemic rating means it won't mess with your blood sugar.

4. **Cucumbers-** Hydrate and replenish your skin with fresh cucumbers. In addition to containing 95 percent water, cucumbers are rich in anti-inflammatory compounds that help remove waste from the body and reduce skin irritation. Preliminary research also suggests cucumbers promote anti-wrinkling and anti-aging activity in the skin.

5. **Watermelon-** No surprise here — "water" is in the name, after all. Watermelon flesh contains 91 percent water. This summer treat also contains abundant lycopene, which can help protect cells from sun damage and improve your complexion.

6. **Cauliflower-** Surprised? Well, cauliflower is actually 92 percent water by weight. It's rich in vitamin C, vitamin K, and other key essentials. Cauliflower and other cruciferous vegetables contain nutrients that may help lower cholesterol and lower cancer risk. Try it mashed or roasted for a yummy substitute to potatoes.

7. **Grapefruit-** contains only 30 calories and is comprised of 90 percent water. Phytonutrients called limonoids, found in grapefruits, can be detoxifying and may inhibit tumor formation of cancers.

8. **Coconut water-** is comprised of 95 percent water. It is one of the most popular ways to hydrate the moderate-intensity athlete. Coconut water differs from coconut milk because it is found in young coconuts only.

Make sure to always choose organic and add 1-2 new veggies or fruits to your next meal.

And of course, you need to know…

How Much
Should I Eat?

All your meals should follow the magic plate guidelines when creating your own meals. The chart below shows you how to measure portion sizes without a food scale. This method is to be followed for the duration of the 28-day reset.

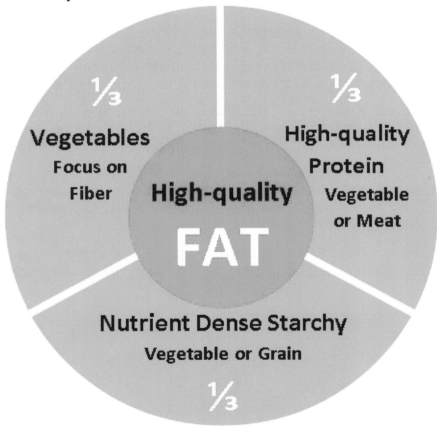

Serving Guidelines

Animal Sources
1 serving = 3oz or the size of your palm.

Dried Beans
¼ to ½ cup maximum

Nuts / Seeds
¼ cup maximum

Veggies
1 cup cooked or raw.

Grains
¼ to ½ cup maximum

Fruits
½ cup maximum

Oils / Fats
1 to 3 tsp

Will I be hungry?

You shouldn't be hungry on this reset but if you are... ask yourself, what am I hungry for?

Make sure you note this observation in your JOURNAL, either your own or the one in this book!

Cultivate a BIG curiosity about what drives you to eat, especially outside of mealtimes.

Make sure you are prepping meals when you are mildly hungry vs. starving. Honor your fullness by completing your meal when you are at a 7 on the Hunger & Fullness Speedometer out of 10.

What this means is eating to be energized, but still having room in your belly.

If you are feeling the compulsion to continue to eat beyond a 7, pause, tell your body you will eat again later, that this meal or snack is complete, have a cup of tea and engage in a reset enhancing, non-food activity.

"Those who don't believe in magic will never find it"

- Roald Dahl

Honoring Hunger & Fullness

If you want to build healthy habits around food, what you eat is only part of the big picture. We also must look at:

- HOW we eat
- Who are you "being" when you eat?
- Do you eat when you're not actually hungry?
- Do you eat too little or too much?

This is very important when trying to conceive because the main cause of infertility is PCOS or high blood sugar. Keeping your meals consistent and only eating until you are 80% full will keep your blood sugar stable throughout the day and will help you manage or reverse the signs and symptoms associated with PCOS.

How do we "Honor Hunger"?

- Tune into your internal signal that the body needs nourishment.
- Recognize hunger - learn the signs.
- Create an intuitive inner speedometer.
- You always want to stay in the neutral or satisfied category, so your hunger scale is balanced, and you are satisfied.
- Start planning what to eat when that needle starts to dip.
- Once you hit the hungry mark, it is too late and that is when bad choices are made.

How do we "Honor Fullness"?

- The same goes for fullness.
- You always want to keep the needle in the middle and on satisfied when you start to become overfull or stuffed, it is very unpleasant.
- Aim for nourished and energized, satiated but not stuffed, bloated or nauseous.

Logically, the hunger & fullness speedometer makes sense.

Here's the problem – most of us have habits of eating beyond fullness. So, let's create some new habits around honoring hunger and fullness.

1. Start planning what and when to eat when your speedometer slightly dips.
2. Eat high-energy foods that your body wants.
3. Eat for energy satisfied but not stuffed.
4. Make a physical gesture that your meal is complete by pushing your plate away, putting a napkin over it, or crossing silverware.
5. Declare out loud to yourself or whomever you are eating with that you are full. This will dissuade you from continuing to eat because you've already announced that the meal was complete for you.
6. If you're out, ask your server to box up the rest of the meal so it's not calling you hither.

My Intuitive Inner Hunger & Fullness Speedometer

This week, I'll prepare for food when my Inner Speedometer starts to dip.

This week, I'll practice completing my meal when my Inner Speedometer is on satisfied but not stuffed.

Action Steps –

Your action steps for the week are preparing to start the Reset Phases 1 & 2.

Pay attention to your body and journal any feelings that come up. Know that it is completely normal to feel tired, emotional, or not yourself but this is all normal. Your body is working very hard to release toxins and create an optimal environment for baby-making.

AHA - What are your "ahas" and appreciations for this week. Let's end on a positive note.

Write these down and be proud of all your accomplishments big or small. You got this mama. I am so proud of you.

Journal Prompt –

Time I feel hungry- _____ _____

What am I doing/working on right now?

_____
_____
_____
_____

Is there something I am wanting to avoid, procrastinate or distract myself away from?

_____
_____
_____
_____

What I want right now is...

_____
_____
_____
_____

How I am choosing to honor my body is…

_____
_____
_____
_____

Reset Checklist

This is a resource to use on your fridge or somewhere you will see it, to make sure you are following through with everything you need to do on this reset.

Day	1	2	3	4	5	6	7	8	9	10	11	12	13	14
Hot Water with Lemon														
Flax Cocktail AM PM														
12 Hour Over-Night Fast (note hours)														
Deep Breathing														
Dry Skin Brushing														
Detox Tea														
Enema														
Hours of Sleep														
Cleanse Enhancing Activities														
Fullness Scale (1-10)														
Movement														

How to Go Dairy-Free Cheat Sheet

Why Should I Consider Going Dairy-Free?

Dairy products contain casein, whey, and lactose. Any one of those three may cause problems within the digestive system. If you have digestive challenges, it may be worth trying a dairy-free diet for 7-14 days to see if symptoms are reduced.

How Do I Go Dairy-Free?

Products to avoid:

- Any cow-based dairy products including whole milk, low-fat milk, 1% milk, skim milk, all cheese varieties, sour cream, puddings, ice creams, frozen yogurt, and yogurt
- Goat-based, sheep-based and camel-based dairy products including milk, cheese, ice creams, and yogurts

Here is a list of alternatives that do not naturally contain casein, whey, or lactose.

Dairy Milk Alternatives:

- Soy Milk
- Rice Milk
- Hemp Milk
- Almond Milk
- Coconut Milk (So Delicious for cereal/cooking and canned, for recipes requiring a fattier version)
- Flax Milk (Good Karma)
- Cashew Milk (Silk)

Dairy Cheese Alternatives: NOTE: Always double-check the ingredient label for casein and sodium caseinate since these are common additives even in non-dairy alternatives

- Rice milk cheese slices
- Almond milk cheese slices
- Daiya is a popular vegan choice and it melts well

Dairy Yogurt Alternatives:

- o Soy yogurt
- o Coconut yogurt
- o Almond yogurt

Dairy Butter Alternatives:

- o Earth Balance vegan spread
- o Olive oil
- o Avocado oil
- o Coconut butter

Dairy Ice cream Alternatives:

- o Almond ice cream (Almond Dream)
- o Coconut ice cream (So Delicious brand)
- o Rice Ice cream (Rice Dream)
- o Soy ice cream
- o Frozen bananas, berries, mangos, pineapples, etc. also make great alternatives if you have a high-powered blender or food processor

Other Dairy Alternative items:

- o Puddings – there are dairy-free options on the market now such as ZenSoy, or you can make your own at home using canned coconut milk.
- o Creamers – Soy and coconut-based creamers are widely available at most grocery stores
- o Sour cream – Soy-based versions are the most commonly available. I would avoid unless you can't live without it.

What about butter?

Great question! Glad you asked! Most people who need to or choose to avoid dairy can tolerate butter. However, there are exceptions to this rule and alternatives. Thank goodness! Butter contains trace amounts of casein. There is a casein-free version known as ghee. This isn't a brand, it's the name of the food. Ghee is a type of clarified butter and is made by heating butter and then straining the liquid through cheesecloth or another filter. The casein can be thrown away or re-used by those that tolerate it. You can make this at home or purchase it at a grocery store. There are many ways, some quite complex, to make ghee so you might find certain types preferable to others.

Making ghee at home –

Take several sticks of butter (preferably from grass-fed cows) and place them in a slow cooker for 1.5-2 hours. When the butter is all liquid, you can strain it with cheesecloth into a glass container with a cover.

Storing ghee –

Ghee is stored like butter. If you leave it in the fridge, it will get hard (it actually gets harder than regular butter). If you leave it on the counter, it will go bad faster but be softer. Most people leave it in the fridge and take it out just prior to use.

Using ghee –

You can use ghee just like you would have used butter. You can spoon it, spread it, cook with it, or throw it in your coffee or tea.

Making the decision to go dairy-free during trying to conceive can make a huge difference in your health, the blood sugar roller coaster and how you feel. Try going dairy-free today and see how you feel.

The "How To" Coffee Guide

(...including how to quit if you want)

Facts About Caffeine in Coffee

- One cup of coffee has somewhere between 75-150 mg of caffeine.
- Caffeine occurs naturally in coffee and is enhanced during the roasting process.

Health Benefits of Coffee

- Caffeine stimulates the nervous system and the brain and can fight fatigue and increase athletic performance.
- Caffeine may also help with headaches and migraine pain.
- Coffee is loaded with antioxidants made of quinines, which become more potent after roasting.
- Magnesium is found naturally in coffee; when magnesium is combined with quinines, we see a lowering effect on blood sugar that may be responsible for a lower risk of type II diabetes development.
- Coffee contains the antibacterial compound trigonelline, which may help in the prevention of dental caries (cavities). This compound becomes more pronounced during roasting and is also responsible for giving coffee its unforgettable aroma.
- Researchers are drawing a strong connection (correlation) between coffee and its potential preventative measures of Parkinson's disease.
- Coffee may also lower the incidence of liver cancer and liver disease.
    - Researchers noted a reduction of liver cancer risk by about 50% in those who drank 3 cups of coffee per day.
    - Coffee showed an ability to reduce alcoholic cirrhosis by about 22%
    - Coffee consumption reduced mortality from cirrhosis due to alcohol by 66%

If Coffee Is So Healthy, Then Why Aren't We Seeing the Benefits?

Last year, according to coffeeresearch.org, Americans consume approximately 4.4 kg of coffee per person annually. This equates to roughly 3.1 cups of coffee per day per person!

So why aren't Americans seeing the health benefits listed above?

Two main reasons:

1. The quality of coffee
2. What we put in coffee

The Quality of Coffee Pesticide Concerns

o Coffee shows up on many lists of products that are very high in pesticides. The agrochemicals are directed at the stems and leaves, but independent tests are finding residue on the beans themselves.
o Roasting only removes partial amounts of the pesticides.
o Pesticides have been linked to endocrine disorders, cancers, and neurological disorders.

Because many types of coffees are imported, the USDA has limited control over the types of pesticides, amounts, and techniques used.

Choose Organic –

o While organic coffee is typically more expensive, the health care costs for the aforementioned conditions are much greater.
o By choosing an organic coffee you are not only improving your own health, but the health of the coffee farmers and the condition of the land on which the plants are grown.

Other Notable Coffee Trends –

o Shade-grown: Coffee is grown in a manner that protects rainforests. Shade-grown coffee farmers will plant their coffee crops under another crops such as avocados or citrus trees. Shade-grown coffee connoisseurs tout that this type of coffee is more robust and flavorful than the full-sun-grown counterparts.
o Fair-trade: Fair-trade was created in the effort to promote a more amicable trading environment to ensure that producers in developing countries are paid a fair price for products while increasing sustainability. *Grounds for Change* coffee is an example of fair-trade, organic and shade-grown coffee. Almost half of organic coffee is also labeled as fair-trade.

- UTZ-certified: Signifies that the coffee was grown under fair labor practices with as minimal chemical application as possible. It is traceable from farmer to roaster to consumer and emphasizes transparency.

The Quality of Decaf Coffee –

Decaffeinated coffee contains 10 mg or less of caffeine, versus 75-150mg in a regular cup of coffee.

To remove the caffeine from coffee, producers use numerous chemicals like benzene, high levels of carbon dioxide and methyl chloride, most of which are carcinogenic.

If you must drink decaf, choose a brand that uses steam extraction such as the Swiss Water Process®.

What We Put in Coffee –

Chemicals, Creamers, and Sugars… Oh My!

In addition to the pesticide and carcinogen concerns discussed above, there are 2 more components we put in coffee that keeps us from experiencing its health benefits.

1) **Sweeteners & Artificial Sweeteners**

   a) Sweeteners: Putting poor-quality sweeteners in coffee adds unwanted chemicals AND calories. Case in point – Starbucks most popular blended coffee drinks rack up about 500-750 calories per 16-ounce serving. Most of that is sugar, which converts in the body to fat.

   b) Artificial sweeteners: Add to the chemical load of the body, convert into other more carcinogenic substances during the body's own detoxification process, and increase the carbohydrate cravings.

2) Poor Quality Dairy

Most creamers or coffee lighteners that are sold as such are some of the lowest quality dairy products on the market.

a) Whole Milk

    i) Contains lactose, casein, and whey for those who may be intolerant

    ii) High fat content

    iii) Triggers growth hormone production in the human body

    iv) May have added hormones and/or antibiotics from dairy cows

    v) If you need to use a liquid coffee lightener, choose organic whole milk

b) Low-fat Milk/1% Milk/Skim Milk

    i) Contains lactose, casein, and whey for those who may be intolerant

    ii) Triggers growth hormone production in the human body

    iii) May have added hormones and/or antibiotics from dairy cows

    iv) May contain chemical additives to replace the removed fat

c) Non-Dairy Creamer

    i) Typically made of partially hydrogenated oils (trans fats), casein, corn syrup solids, soybean, canola and/or sunflower oils, artificial flavors and colors, etc. (basically a storm of chemicals).

    ii) While "non-dairy" creamer does not contain lactose, it does contribute to the overall inflammatory process of the body because it increases arachidonic acid production in the body. Avoid.

d) Flavored Creamers

    i) Flavored creamers such as Coffee-Mate are generally chemical nightmares that contribute to systemic inflammation

    ii) They often contain:

        (1) Corn syrup solids – triggers insulin response and may lead to insulin resistance

(2) Vegetable oil (including partially hydrogenated soybean and/or cottonseed oil) – trans-fatty acids that may lead to heart disease and/or stroke

(3) Sodium caseinate – triggers opioid centers in the brain increasing desire to consume more

(4) Dipotassium phosphate – a fertilizer that is used to prevent clumping

(5) Sodium aluminosilicate – contains aluminum which has been connected to the development of such conditions as Alzheimer's disease - Artificial flavor depending on the type purchased

The Highest-Quality Coffee –

- Organic, fair trade, shade-grown
  Drink black or add:

    - *A TBSP of Kerrygold unsalted grass-fed butter and/ or some coconut oil or MCT (medium chain triglyceride) oil.*

        - If you blend coffee, butter, and oil, coffee will get frothy and taste like a richer, healthier latte

        - Google Dave Asprey's "Bulletproof Coffee" for more information

    - Sweeten with flavored or plain liquid stevia.

- Also adding pure vanilla extract or other pure flavored extracts will help naturally flavor your coffee.

Should I Quit Drinking Coffee?

While we've seen that coffee does have health benefits, the amount of caffeine that is present in coffee may be causing problems in your body.

If you have any of the following health challenges or concerns, you may want to consider reducing or eliminating coffee and caffeine.

Adrenal Fatigue

One of the major health challenges from coffee consumption is exhausted adrenal glands.

Since caffeine stimulates the Central Nervous System, or CNS, it causes the adrenal glands to secrete the hormone adrenaline. Adrenaline signals the body to stay in a constant state of readiness, which also means a constant stress response.

Eventually, the adrenal glands cannot sustain the stress response and they fatigue.

This is a serious problem because the adrenal glands are essential in regulating youth and sex hormones such as DHEA, pregnenolone, progesterone, testosterone, and estrogen.

As adrenals fatigue even further, thyroid function and other crucial metabolic systems can be affected.

Drinking coffee on an empty stomach can also affect your hormones so unless you are having bulletproof coffee which has the healthy fats you need, eat breakfast first and then have your coffee.

Blood Sugar Imbalance (aka Blood Sugar Roller Coaster)

Caffeine also forces the liver to release glycogen into the blood, creating a sudden increase in blood sugar. This forces the pancreas to respond by secreting insulin in response to the increased blood sugar.

Therefore, repeated consumption of caffeine can trigger the Blood Sugar Roller Coaster, which can lead to weight gain, insulin resistance, diabetes and a host of other health concerns.

Coffee can also inhibit the absorption of some nutrients and increases urinary excretion of magnesium, iron, potassium, calcium and trace minerals. This can increase the risk of the development of osteoporosis.

Pregnancy, Fertility, PMS, & Hormones

Pregnant women really need to be careful of their caffeine intake since caffeine can cross the placenta and can increase the risk of miscarriage. It can also increase infertility in those who are trying to conceive. Fibrocystic breast disease and PMS symptoms can be made worse by caffeine consumption and may increase hormonal fluctuations during menopause.

Urinary Irritation & Dehydration

Coffee is also an irritant to the urinary tract, including the bladder. For those who suffer from frequent urination, coffee acts as a diuretic. For men who have enlarged prostate glands, it would be a good idea to eliminate coffee and caffeine to reduce the associated symptoms and frequent urination.

Although coffee contains water, it actually forces the body to excrete more water than coffee can provide, so it is dehydrating instead of hydrating.

Heart Conditions

Those with heart conditions, especially irregular heartbeat, need to be concerned with their coffee consumption. Since coffee has the ability to excrete magnesium and calcium – two major regulatory minerals for heart muscle functioning – coffee consumption can further dysregulate the heart.

Vitamin & Mineral Absorption Challenges

Magnesium is also essential for the breakdown of fats in the body. Without efficient breakdown of fats, the body is also unable to utilize the fat-soluble vitamins A, D, E and K, so they are also excreted more quickly than normal.

Coffee can also lead to B and C vitamin deficiencies. B-vitamin deficiency (in particular B6, folate and B12) can be particularly dangerous since they help to control the levels of homocysteine in the body.

How Do I Quit Drinking Coffee Without Losing My Mind?
- Gradually dilute your coffee until you are consuming only hot water.
- Start with 90% coffee and 10% water. Keep this ratio for a week or more.
- Next, reduce the coffee to 75% and increase water to 25% of your cup. Again, keep this ratio for a week or more.
- Now you can go quicker! For four days, try a half and half coffee-to-water mixture.
- Let coffee go and switch to hot water with lemon

Additional Strategies –

- o Switch from coffee to green tea and follow the reduction schedule above. Green tea has approximately 25 mg of caffeine per cup compared to coffee's 75-150mg per cup.
- o Ginseng can help keep you in balance during caffeine withdrawal. Caffeine constricts blood vessels and ginseng dilates them. Be sure to take ginseng BEFORE
- o the onset of a headache. Follow label directions.
- o Consider switching to herbal teas such as dandelion tea. This tastes like coffee, but also adds liver cleansing benefits.
- o Try coffee alternatives, like Dandy Blend or Teccino (made with barley but has no detectable amount of gluten).
- o Make sure to drink at least 6-8 glasses of filtered water daily. This helps to keep you hydrated and helps the bowels eliminate. This is especially important for those who tend toward constipation.
- o Make sure you get 8 hrs of sleep every night. Also, try afternoon 20-min power naps to increase energy and productivity.
- o Exercise! Even if you can only fit in 30 minutes of walking during a lunch break it will do wonders for your energy (plus it will help get bowels moving).
- o Eat regular meals with high-quality protein, fat, and fiber to keep your blood sugar and your energy steady.
- o Avoid eating until too full: eating too much will create tension and tightness in your digestive system, which will make you crave the lightening effects of coffee. Eat until satisfied, or about 80% full.
- o Try right-nostril breathing. Pinch off the left nostril and breathe exclusively through the right for a few minutes each day. This helps create a natural stimulant by increasing oxygen flow. This may mimic the caffeine effect.

References

National Coffee Association of U.S.A. The History of Coffee.

http://ncausa.org

Coffee is the number one source of antioxidants.

http://www.prnewswire.com/newsreleases

Goto A, Song Y, Chen BH, et al. Coffee and caffeine consumption in relation to sex hormone-binding globulin and risk of type 2 diabetes in postmenopausal women. Diabetes. 2011 Jan;60(1):269-75.

Ross GW, Abbott RD, Petrovitch H, et al. Association of coffee and caffeine intake with the risk of Parkinson disease. JAMA. 2000 May 24-31;283(20):2674-9.

Bravi F, Bosetti C, Tavani A, Gallus S, La Vecchia C. Coffee reduces risk for hepatocellular carcinoma: an updated meta-analysis. Clin Gastroenterol Hepatol. 2013 Nov;11(11):14131421.e1.

Klatsky AL, Morton C, Udaltsova N, Friedman GD. Coffee, cirrhosis, and transaminase enzymes. Arch Intern Med. 2006 Jun 12;166(11):1190-5.

Telles S, Nagarathna R, Nagendra HR. Breathing through a particular nostril can alter metabolism and autonomic activities. Indian J Physiol Pharmacol. 1994 Apr;38(2):133-7.

Your Fertility Reset Daily Schedule

Rise and shine- breakfast

Upon rising drink an 8oz glass of warm lemon water. Follow with a flaxseed cocktail. During the next 15 minutes breathe, stretch, walk outside, skin brush and bathe, end with a cool rinse. Eat breakfast and detox tea (after you eat).

Mid-Morning

Snack, if needed, fruit, veggies, a small handful of nuts. Breathe. Drink water. You got this!

Mid-day lunch

Enjoy your lunch, have some detox tea, if the weather permits, sun gaze (stand outside and gaze at the sun with your eyes closed, feel the warm sunlight on the backs of your eyelids.) or a 5 min meditation.

Late afternoon

Snack, if needed, fruit, veggies, nuts. Breathe. Drink water. Belly massage. Connect to support.

Evening/Dinner (before 7)

Drink warm water with lemon 20 minutes before dinner, then have dinner with some detox tea. Do any support activities ex: breathe, gentle exercise, walk, skin brush, and bathe (if you didn't do it in the morning). Complete your last meal by 7 pm. Your body needs about 12 hours to fully reset and recover.

Sample Grocery List

Meat/poultry/fish

- 1 package of organic chicken breasts
- 2 freshwater salmon filets
- 2 freshwater halibut filets
- 1 package tofu

Grains and beans

- 1 box rice cereal
- 1 package quinoa
- 1 bag dried lentils
- 1 loaf rice bread

non-dairy milk and broths

- 1-gallon unsweetened almond milk
- 1 bottle coconut water unsweetened
- 1 no sodium added vegetable broth
- 2 cans full-fat coconut milk (unsweetened)

Fruits

- 1 bag frozen cherries/blueberries
- 2 mangos
- 3 limes
- 1 lemon
- 3 apples
- 2 peaches

Nuts and seeds

- 1 bag raw almonds
- 1 bag raw pumpkin seeds 1 bag raw sunflower seeds 1 bag unsweetened coconut milk 1 bag ground flax seeds

Vegetables

- 1 bag spinach
- 1 bunch dino kale
- 2 scallions
- 2 medium leeks
- 1 parsnip
- 5 avocados
- 1 bag carrots
- 1 purple cabbage
- 1 zucchini
- 1 bag celery stalks
- 1 box mushrooms
- 1 bunch kale
- 1 red pepper
- 1 white onion
- 3 butternut squash 1 bag romaine lettuce leaves

NOTES

NOTES

NOTES

Client Testimonial   - **Tiffany and Brian T.**

When this couple came to me, they were broken, emotional and just couldn't think of moving forward with their fertility fight. They had tried everything from 3 rounds of Clomid, 2 unsuccessful IVF rounds and were about to go into the 3 round of IVF and were starting the trigger shots next week. Tiffany was heartbroken and emotional. She didn't understand why nothing was working when the doctors told her and her husband "nothing was wrong with them".

They knew they didn't want to keep going down this road, but they desperately wanted a baby.

That is when they were referred to me by their doctor. Their doctor knew there was nothing medically wrong and traditional fertility treatments weren't working.

They decided to try a more holistic approach and enrolled in my program. We made some simple tweaks to both their diets and lifestyles. Incorporating simple action steps that they could both do daily that would boost their fertility and were WAY less painful and invasive than what they had been doing.

After about 3 months, guess what… they got pregnant. They couldn't believe it and were ecstatic.

Will you be next?

Chapter 4

Re-introduction Puzzle Piece

*This chapter is compatible with **Week 3** of The Hormone Puzzle Online Coaching program. *

(www.hormonepuzzle.com)

Hey gorgeous! Welcome back. You have made it to week 3. Congrats. How did last week go? I hope the reset went well for you. Write in your journal, how it went. Were you consistent? What toxins were you able to release? How are you starting to feel? Let's get this all out of your head and onto paper. I find this helps me to reboot and recharge when I can see the actual progress being made. Great job.

You never know how strong you are until being strong is the only choice you have

- Bob Marley

This week we are going to talk about reintroduction. The reason I am having you reintroduce is because…

…some foods taste great, but leave you feeling terrible.

They can cause mood swings, digestive upset, bloating and fatigue. I want you to get clear on which foods trigger toxic symptoms which will help you steer your health and create an optimal environment for a healthy pregnancy and baby.

During the reset this week you will use your journal to record any reactions you might have. Pay attention to how you feel shortly after eating each re-introduced food item. Do you have a runny nose or mucus in the throat, fatigue, bloating or a headache? How is your energy, your emotions, brain function, sleep, skin, bowels, etc? All of these are symptoms of an allergy or intolerance. Even the smallest reaction can send big signals to your body and reproductive organs that it isn't safe to create life and therefore you don't get pregnant.

Once you learn which foods you react to you can decide if you want to include them in your diet or not.

The way reintroduction works- first decide which foods you want to reintroduce. If you weren't eating a food before the reset, don't reintroduce. Only do this with the foods you want in your diet.

Most people start with gluten or dairy.

But you can start with any food listed on the re-introduction list, or you can pick your own based on known allergens. You will add the food to your meals 1-2 times per day which you continue to eat the reset menu.

So, if you add gluten that could look like toast for breakfast or a sandwich for lunch.

The main thing to remember is you want to isolate that food to see if it causes a reaction and then record those reactions on the handout in the resources section of this chapter.

Once you reintroduce the targeted food for 2 days then you have a day in between to let your body reset and then you do it with another food again for 2 days. You can continue this reintroduction diet until you have reintroduced any known allergen and recorded your results.

Now that you have cleaned your body by detoxing and resetting and you have determined which foods cause allergies or irritate you, you can move into a more targeted eating plan.

You will continue to eat based on the magic plate.

Choosing high-quality foods that give you energy and don't cause allergy or irritation.

In my 1-1 coaching, I go into more specifics about which foods to eat and we work together to create menus around which foods work for your body and blood type, which foods are known allergens to you and which foods are going to put you in the optimal state of conceiving.

However, for the purposes of this workbook and course, I am giving you the power to create your own menus. You now should know how to do this based on what you learned during the reset, which foods cause allergies and how to construct a magic plate.

Remember we want to focus on the magic plate -

⅓ vegetable, ⅓ high-quality-protein, ½ cruciferous vegetable (fiber) and 1-2 TBSP of high-quality fat.

Re-introduction

3 RE-INTRODUCTION (5 DAYS)

Learning About Irritants & Intolerances

Some foods taste great but leave you feeling terrible. They can cause mood swings, digestive upset, bloating and fatigue. Getting clear on which foods trigger toxic symptoms will help you steer your health.

You will use your journal to record any reactions you might have.

Pay attention to how you feel shortly after eating each re-introduced food item. Do you have a runny nose or mucus in the throat (typical of milk), or fatigue, bloating, or a headache (typical of wheat)?

Energy

How are your energy levels? A bowl of wheat pasta at night, for example, may make you feel very tired immediately after eating it or upon waking the next morning.

Emotion

How do you feel emotionally the next day? Are you anxious, angry, moody, depressed or irritable?

Bowels

How are your movements the next day? Were they as frequent and as easy to eliminate as they were during the cleanse or do you feel cramping, pain or gas, constipation or diarrhea?

Brain Function

How are you functioning? Do you have headaches, suffering from foggy brain? Are you having any issues concentrating?

Sleep

Did you have difficulty falling or staying asleep? Did you have intense dreams or nightmares? Did you wake up in the middle of the night?

Skin / Congestion

Do you notice any skin breakouts? Are you experiencing a runny nose or mucus in the throat?

We will focus on reintroducing the two most common irritants:

Gluten & Dairy

Step 1: Adding in gluten 2 to 3 times a day for 2 days

You'll still be following the re-set diet; the only difference is that you'll now be adding in gluten to see how your body reacts to it. If you weren't eating gluten before or have known food issues, don't reintroduce! How to: Try adding bread to your breakfast, and then some pasta for lunch or dinner. Don't include any dairy or other excluded items yet. The goal is to isolate one excluded food at a time to determine if you are intolerant or sensitive. Take notes. Not everyone will react to gluten in the same way. You may notice reactions immediately... or reactions the next day. That's why it's important to test gluten over the course of two days.

Step 2: Clean the slate

After you have re-introduced gluten it's important to "clean the slate" and set your body up for testing the next possible irritant. You need to follow the reset diet for 2 days to allow your body to recover.

Step 3: Adding in dairy 2 to 3 times a day for 1 to 2 days

If you weren't eating dairy before or have known food issues, don't reintroduce! How to: Try having a glass of milk in the morning and a few pieces of cheese with your lunch or evening meal. It's important to avoid having dairy in combination with other excluded foods. Take notes. Examples: I felt bloated and gassy; I felt tired; I felt itchy etc.

Step 4: Adding in other common irritants

Go slowly and take good notes... add one item at a time. Start with processed sugar, then caffeine, alcohol, etc.

The Magic Plate

Healthy Meals at a Glance

1/3
Vegetables
Focus on Fiber

1/3
High-quality Protein
Vegetable or Meat

High-quality FAT

Nutrient Dense Starchy
Vegetable or Grain
1/3

Magic Snacks

1. 2 TBSP hazelnut butter and an apple
2. 2 TBSP almond butter, ½ cup celery, optional: sprinkle 1 TBSP chia seeds in almond butter
3. 2oz pulled chicken, ½ cup avocado mixed together
4. ½ cup raspberries, 1-2 TBSP of homemade whipped cream with a sprinkle of pumpkin seeds.
5. ¼ cup black beans, ¼ cup salsa, ½ cup avocado
6. ½ cup raspberries, ½ cup cottage cheese
7. 1oz cheddar cheese, ½ pear, 12 almonds
8. ½ cup sweet potato, ¼ cup full-fat plain yogurt or sour cream
9. ½ cup squash, 1 TBSP butter, 1 TBSP ground flax seed sprinkles on top
10. ½ cup roasted chickpeas, with cinnamon
11. 2 TBSP cashew butter, ½ banana, ¼ cup dry oatmeal. Mix together and enjoy!
12. ½ apple, 2 TBSP almond butter, chia seeds sprinkled on top
13. 1 tomato cut into slices, ½ cup mashed avocado layered on top of tomato slices, 1oz shredded cheese sprinkled as the final layer. Broil on baking sheet for a couple of minutes.
14. ½ cup hummus, ½ cup celery or carrots, a small handful of high fiber crackers
15. 1 hardboiled egg sliced on crackers or high fiber bread, 1 TBSP mayo
16. 2 TBSP shredded coconut, ¼ cup dry oats, ½ banana. Mix together and enjoy!
17. 1 pear, 12 almonds
18. ½ cup roasted brussels sprouts with 1-2 TBSP of olive oil sprinkled with turmeric, ginger and cinnamon.
19. Quinoa tabbouleh (1/2 cup cooked quinoa, 2 TBSP chopped onion, ½ of a diced tomato, 1-2 TBSP olive oil, ½ TBSP fresh squeezed lemon, 1 TBSP feta cheese and mint, salt and pepper to taste)
20. ½ cup cooked whole-grain pasta of choice (like brown rice, red lentil or whole wheat), 2 TBSP basil pesto, 2oz fresh mozzarella cheese. Mix together and enjoy warm or cold!
21. 3 frozen dates and an apple
22. ½ cup plain yogurt, ½ cup berries of choice, ground flax seeds mixed in
23. ½ cup homemade trail mix with almonds, cashews, sunflower seeds, Craisins, and some dark chocolate nibs
24. ½ cup bell peppers sliced wrapped in 2oz prosciutto with a side of 5 olives
25. ½ cup almond milk, 2 TBSP seed mix (chia, hemp, flax), ½ cup berries all mixed in a bowl

Serving Guidelines

Animal sources- 1 serving = 3oz or the size of your palm

Dried beans - ¼- ½ cup max

Nuts / Seeds - ¼ cup max

Vegetables - 1 cup cooked or raw

Grains - ¼ - ½ cup max

Fruits - ½ cup or 1 piece

Oils / Fats - 1-3 TBSP

Hungry –

You shouldn't be hungry on this fertility reset but if you are… ask yourself, what am I hungry for?

Make sure you *note this observation in your journal.* Cultivate a BIG curiosity about what drives you to eat, especially outside of mealtimes.

Make sure you are prepping meals when you are mildly hungry vs starving and honor your hunger & fullness speedometer.

Eat for energy but make sure you still have room in your belly. If you are feeling the compulsion to continue to eat beyond fullness, pause, tell your body you will eat again later, that this meal or snack is complete.

Then do a non-food activity that you love, have a cup of tea, or engage in a cleanse enhancing non-food activity until the feeling passes.

You got this mamma! I know you can do it.

Fat, Fat, and Fat – Let's talk about fat

Please see your Reset recipe guide in the recipes section at the back of this book. This will be your manual of recipes for the reset.

After you have completed your re-introduction, we are going to concentrate on adding fat.

This week we are really going to concentrate on adding FAT. FAT, FAT and more healthy fats into our diets. This is an incredible building block for mama and baby.

Eating a diet rich in "good" fats provides a woman with the necessary precursors for healthy hormone levels needed for optimal fertility (there's currently a trend of women struggling with fertility and miscarriages who have low cholesterol levels, i.e. a total less than 160 mg/dl). Including healthy fats in the diet is also critical as it provides the necessary building blocks for developing a healthy fetal brain which happens very early on in the pregnancy.

Adequate cholesterol levels may also help prevent secondary infertility (a woman trying to get pregnant a second time after having had her first child).

Examples: DHA Omega 3 Fatty acids are essential – focus on eating fatty wild-caught cold-water fish

(S.M.A.S.H – Salmon, Mackerel, Anchovy, Sardine, and Herring)

Grass-fed, pasture-raised animal protein such as beef and lamb in particular. Eggs are recommended as well because they are a complete protein (meaning they have all the essential amino acids in one food, and are also high in Choline – a very important vitamin for fetal development which prevents neural-tube defects.)

Never give up on a dream just because of the time it will take to accomplish it

- Earl Nightingale

For so many years low-fat and fat-free was all the rage and people especially women began eliminating or greatly reducing this important macronutrient from their diets in hopes of losing weight or lowering cholesterol. The problem is our bodies need healthy fats to survive and thrive and especially, to create a healthy baby and carry that baby to term. Babies' brains are made of fat so the more fat in your diet the more fuel you will provide for your growing baby's brain.

Here are a few tips on how to bring back the FAT!

1. Incorporate lamb into your diet- Lamb, especially Icelandic lamb if you can get it, has an incredibly high fat content almost 30% higher than beef.

2. Try eating sheep and buffalo milk cheese- Buffalo's milk contains a whooping 10% fat while sheep's milk contains a solid 7% fat, this compared to the 3.4% found in cow's milk.

3. Ditch skim milk and use grass-fed cream in your coffee

4. Sautee, roast, and cook with tallow (rendered beef fat) and lard (rendered pork fat)- make sure to buy quality rendered fats from your butcher.

5. Drink bone broth- this nourishing liquid contains all the minerals, fats, and nutrients for the bones and connective tissues of the animal. It is very nourishing and soothing for the digestive system. Find the recipe in my cookbook – The Complete Hormone Puzzle Cookbook – found on amazon

6. Bulletproof your coffee- Add a TBSP of grass-fed butter and MCT (coconut oil) to your coffee and blend. Fat will temper the caffeine uptake for a "slow burn" energy boost. And no, you don't have to give up your coffee during conception. Just be sure it's organic since it's one of the highest pesticide laden crops in the world and limit your intake to 1-2 8oz cups per day.

7. Skip the more popular lean cuts and try braising/stewing fatty cuts of meat-short ribs, chuck and shanks are good options. Shank cuts will include bone marrow, a delicious and supremely nutritious source of fat- try starting with a simple Osso Buco recipe.

Fat and Fiber Suggestions

Fat Suggestions –

1. Avocado - 1 medium is about 240 calories, 24 g fat and 9 g of fiber
2. Coldwater Salmon- 3 oz is 155 calories, 6.9 g fat, 0 g fiber.
3. Pecans - 7 whole, 14 halves, or ¼ cup 196 calories, 20.4 g fat, 2.7 g fiber.
4. Walnuts - 7 whole, 14 halves, or ¼ cup 183 calories, 18 g fat, 2 g fiber.
5. Olive oil – 1 TBSP - 119 calories, 14 g fat, no fiber.
6. Olives- 10 medium olives 115 calories, 10 g fat and no fiber.
7. Dark chocolate – 1oz 155 calories, 9 g fat and 2 g fiber.
8. Chia seeds- 1oz 138 calories, 9 g fat and 10 g fiber.
9. Flax seeds – 1 TBSP, 55 calories, 4 g fat, and 8 g fiber.
10. Full-fat swiss cheese – 1oz 90 calories, 7 g fat and 9 g fiber.

Fiber Suggestions –

1. Pear – 1 medium, 100 calories, 0 g fat, 6 g of fiber
2. Strawberries – 1/2 cup 32 calories, .2 g of fat and 2 g of fiber
3. Avocado - 1 medium is about 240 calories, 24 g fat and 9 g of fiber
4. Apple – 1 medium 93 calories, .3 g of fat and 5 g of fiber
5. Carrots – ½ cup chopped 25 calories, .1 g of fat and 1.7 g of fiber
6. Lentils – 1 cup cooked 240 calories, 0 g fat and 16 g fiber
7. Chickpeas – ¼ cup 200 calories, 3.5 g fat and 9 g fiber
8. Sweet potatoes – 1 medium 114 calories, .1 g fat and 4 g fiber
9. Gluten-free oats – ½ cup 150 calories, 7 g fat and 10 g fiber
10. Almonds – ½ cup 265 calories, 22.5 g fat and 5.5 g fiber

Your action steps for this week are to begin adding 1-3 TBSP of healthy fat with every meal. Use the handout for examples and have fun. Fat is so delicious and leaves you feeling satisfied and happy.

Reset Reintroduction Action Guide

The food I am reintroducing is-

_____

_____

_____

_____

Do I feel- Circle all that apply

Energy Low Medium High Tired Foggy Sluggish Bowels Regular Frequent Infrequent Hard Soft
Cramping Pain Gas Constipation Diarrhea Sleep Trouble falling asleep Trouble staying asleep Insane
dreams Nightmares Restless Emotions Anxious Angry Moody Depressed Irritable Happy Excited
Joyful Grateful Brain Function Headaches Foggy Brain Concentration Issues Daydreaming
Skin/congestion Acne blotchy skin hives runny nose congestion mucus in throat Sore throat

Reset Checklist

Day	1	2	3	4	5	6	7	8	9	10	11	12	13	14
Hot Water with Lemon														
Flax Cocktail AM PM														
12 Hour Over- Night Fast (note hours)														
Deep Breathing														
Dry Skin Brushing														
Detox Tea														
Enema														
Hours of Sleep														
Cleanse Enhancing Activities														
Fullness Scale (1-10)														
Movement														

What are your aha's for this week? Remember I like to end each week with an aha or appreciation about what you learned. Write down the one thing you learned or took away from this session.

Let these words strengthen your bond with yourself and use it as fuel to make a healthy baby and live the life of your dreams.

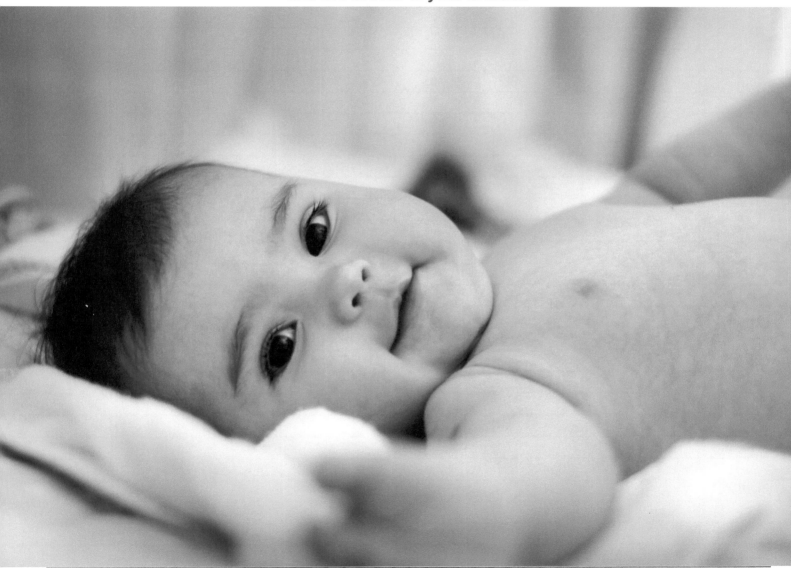

NOTES

NOTES

NOTES

NOTES

Client Testimonial   - **Mandy and Mark F.**

This couple came to me after struggling for about 3 years to get pregnant. Mandy had been struggling with PCOS since she was a teen and was told by doctors that she would probably never get pregnant. Not wanting to hear that advice she decided to take her health into her own hands and got super intentional with what she was eating.

"Coach Kela really helped me to see it wasn't just about eating healthy, but about eating foods that work with my individual body."

After doing my simple action steps over the course of about 6 weeks, Mandy got pregnant and she couldn't be happier or believe that her dreams finally were coming true.

Will you be next?

Chapter 5

Protein and Fiber Puzzle Piece

*This chapter is compatible with **Week 4** of The Hormone Puzzle Online Coaching program. *

(*www.hormonepuzzle.com*)

Hi beautiful, welcome back It's coach Kela your host for this program. It's time to start week 4.

As always let's start our session with what is going well. What went well last week? Let's write that down in our journal.

Were you able to add in healthy fats? Which fats did you add in? How did they make you feel? Were you consistent? Were you able to stick to the magic plate? Did you find any foods that cause allergy or irritation? Were you able to release those and remove them from your diet? Write this all down.

As a reminder, removing these things from your head and onto paper clears it all out and frees the mind and body allowing it to be open for new things and possibilities.

This week we are going to continue to a*dd foods into our diet that promote fertility and optimal health for creating a healthy baby.*

These steps also work well in conjunction with fertility treatments such as clomid, IUI and IVF.

The healthier your body can be the better your chances of conception.

Last week we talked about adding in healthy fats. This week we are going to build on that and add in protein and fiber.

Your mantra should be Fat, Fat, Fat, Protein, Fiber.

These are the building blocks for a healthy baby. You should also concentrate on staying away from any food that causes inflammation especially sugar and processed foods.

Fertility may have challenged us, but we are stronger for it.

Sugar is not only poison to the body, but it sends the emergency signal that we talked about earlier to stop all baby-making processes.

It also hurts our gut bacteria. These bacteria feed on starches. These harm your body's balance while pushing out the good, essential bacteria.

The gut is directly tied to messaging in the brain.

An unhappy gut will ring the alarm to the brain. The largest nerve in the body the vagus nerve, which runs between the brain and the gut and the messaging largely goes from gut to brain, not the other way around.

If the gut bacteria are off thanks to antibiotics killing the good bacteria or too much sugar feeding the bad bacteria, our unhappy gut will send anxious and depressed messaging to the brain.

A distressed brain will not give the signal that it's an ok time to build a baby.

In addition, high blood sugar spiking cortisol means the body will switch over to giving cortisol production the body's B vitamins and essential nutrients instead of building sex hormones to get you pregnant.

Cortisol is such an important hormone for the body to have on hand because of its link to day to day survivability.

The body will always take from other processes to make sure it can make cortisol.

Sticking to fiber-filled fruits as your higher sugar choices, avoids the downsides of processed sugar. Filled with vitamins, minerals, and enzymes, fruit's sugar is negated by its fiber. The presence of fiber drastically helps reduce the sugar spike and therefore damage on hormone balance and insulin issues.

Processed sugar is so dangerous to blood sugar balance and insulin resistance because of the fiber being stripped away in the chemical processing.

We're looking for 30-45 grams of fiber per day and eliminating processed sugar in general.

Fiber acts as an exfoliate for the colon scrubbing it, detoxing, handling blood sugar spikes, and processing extra hormones that tip the balance into the infertile category.

Every meal's focus should be on…

FAT, FIBER, and PROTEIN

"Let your hopes, not your hurts, shape your future."

We're roughly aiming for 20 grams of protein per meal, or 60/day.

Three eggs have 18 grams for instance while a medium handful of nut protein helps us feel full, balances blood sugar, and is made of the amino acid building blocks we need converted into important hormones and brain chemicals.

Protein is another important nutrient with the amino acid building blocks built-in.

Pasture-raised eggs are wonderful pre-pregnancy choices.

A complete protein full of healthy fats will also boast an impressive amount of choline, important Bs, and essential D vitamins. The choline helps avoid dreaded neural tube defects.

20 Sources of High-Quality Protein

1. Eggs – 1 large egg has 6 grams of protein, with 78 calories.
2. Grass-fed beef – One 3 ounce (85 g) serving of cooked beef with 10% fat contains 22 grams of protein, with 184 calories.
3. Free-range chicken – Chicken breast without skin has 6 grams of protein per ounce.
4. Almonds – 6 grams per ounce (28 g), with 161 calories
5. Gluten-free oats- Half a cup of raw oats has 13 grams, with 303 calories.
6. Wild-caught coldwater fish such as Salmon – Salmon is 46% protein, with 19 grams per 3-ounce (85 g) serving and only 175 calories.
7. Wild-caught coldwater Mahi Mahi – 6oz serving, 134 calories and 21gm of protein
8. Non-farmed shrimp – A 3-ounce (85 g) serving contains 18 grams, with only 84 calories.
9. Cottage cheese – A cup (226 g) of cottage cheese with 2% fat contains 27 grams of protein, with 194 calories.
10. Greek yogurt – One 6-ounce (170-gram) container has 17 grams of protein, with only 100 calories.
11. Kefir – 6oz has 100 calories and 6 grams of protein
12. Whole milk – 1 cup of whole milk contains 8 grams of protein, with 149 calories.
13. Broccoli – 1 cup (96 grams) of chopped broccoli has 3 grams of protein, with only 31 calories.
14. Tuna – 94% of calories, in tuna canned in water. A cup (154 g) contains 39 grams of protein, with only 179 calories.
15. Quinoa – One cup (185 g) of cooked quinoa has 8 grams, with 222 calories.
16. Vegan protein shake – my favorite is Sunwarrior. www.sunwarrior.com
    Use my code for 15% off. *Promo code:* **Kelahealth**. Calories – 130 Fat- 3gm Protein 24gm. 1.5 scoop serving size.
17. Lentils – 1 cup (198 g) of boiled lentils contains 18 grams, with 230 calories.
18. Pumpkin seeds – 1 ounce (28 g) has 5 grams of protein, with 125 calories.
19. Salmon – 46% protein, with 19 grams per 3-ounce (85 g) serving and only 175 calories.
20. Peanuts – 1 ounce (28 g) has 7 grams, with 159 calories.

Vitamin D deserves special mention for its many uses in the body. It's is so vital and yet so many of us are desperately low in it. The farther we get from the equator or the more time we spend working inside, the more vitamin D we'll need to get from sources beyond the sun.

Nicknamed the super hormone…

…vitamin D keeps our thyroid healthy putting out cellular energy, mood happy, and both cardiac and immune systems supported.

In summary, ovulation requires nutrients and balanced hormones. Sperm and egg health requires many of these same nutrients. Sugar makes a female body produce male hormones. Cholesterol is a precursor to important hormones and being too low in cholesterol is a huge problem.

The baby's brain is largely made up of healthy fats so make sure mama has enough stored.

This week we are also going to begin to remove gluten from our diet. (if you haven't already). Gluten is a protein prevalent in wheat, barley and rye.

Most foods that contain gluten are highly processed or GMO foods which typically means they are devoid of high-quality nutrients to nourish your body and make a healthy baby.

Gluten also acts like glue on the intestinal tract by "gluing down" the villi that beat to keep the intestinal tract motile and healthy.

The intestinal tract's motility maintains regularity and the villi help absorb nutrients.

Avoiding gluten can lower the overall systemic inflammatory neurological conditions such as depression and schizophrenia since the gut and the brain are deeply connected.

Since so many infertility diagnoses link back to inflammation in the body, PCOS and endometriosis are the top two, it's best to avoid gluten during your fertility journey.

How To Go Gluten-Free Cheat Sheet

What is Gluten?

- Gluten is a protein prevalent in wheat, barley and rye.
- While oats do not contain the gluten protein, they can be cross-contaminated during manufacturing, so select oats specifically labeled gluten-free.

Why Avoid Gluten?

- Most foods that contain gluten are highly processed, which typically means they are devoid of high-quality nutrients to nourish the body.
- Gluten acts like glue on the intestinal tract by "gluing down" the villi that beat to keep the intestinal tract motile and healthy. The intestinal tract's motility maintains regularity and the villi help absorb nutrients.
- Avoiding gluten can lower the overall systemic inflammatory reaction of the body. This may help alleviate or prevent neurological conditions such as depression and schizophrenia since the gut and the brain are deeply interconnected.

How To Avoid Gluten.

- Gluten is easier to avoid than ever before.
- Prepare meals at home with gluten-free ingredients.
- When eating out, research restaurants with gluten-free menus and ask servers to confirm that ingredients in whichever meal you select are gluten-free.
- Put gluten-free snacks in your bag, briefcase or purse so you always have gluten-free food available on the go.

What Do I Do Now?

- Focus on how many delicious foods you CAN eat (versus feeling sad about what you can't).
- Use our Quick-Reference list below to see what you can eat, what you shouldn't, and simple gluten-free swaps.
- Work with your health coach to:
  - Choose a day to gluten-free your pantry and go shopping to restock with gluten-free items.
  - Navigate through any questions you have about whether or not a food is gluten-free.
  - Work through any emotions that come up as you go through this process.
  - Track your progress to determine if your physical symptoms are getting better as a result of eating gluten-free.

Gluten-Free Quick Reference Guide

Foods that are naturally gluten-free:

- ○ Unprocessed/unseasoned meats
- ○ Eggs
- ○ Cheese and other dairy products
- ○ Vegetables
- ○ Fruits
- ○ Nuts and seeds

Check that the nuts and seeds are processed in a facility that is wheat/gluten-free to avoid cross-contamination.

Gluten-free substitutes labeled as such. Examples would be Udi's, Schar, and Glutino brands. Many other companies produce gluten-free foods, but these companies are dedicated gluten-free. Some of the food items they produce include frozen pizzas, pretzels, crackers, tortillas, pie crusts, bread, muffins, cinnamon rolls, etc.

Udi's: http://udisglutenfree.com

Schar: http://www.schar.com

Glutino: http://www.glutino.com

Rice, Amaranth, Millet, Teff are naturally gluten-free grains. Flours are also available in these grains for your personal baking needs.

Alcohol

Gluten-Free beers:

- Steadfast Beer Co. Oatmeal Cream Stout
- Ipswich Ale Brewery: Celia Saison
- Green's Gluten-Free Beers: Enterprise Dry-Hopped Lager
- Sprecher Brewing Co: Shakparo Ale
- Estrella Damm: Daura
- Dogfish Head Craft Brewed Ales: Tweason'ale
- Omission Beer: Lager
- Harvester Brewing IPA No.2 (from Portland, OR)
- Epic Brewing Company: Glutenator (Salt Lake City, UT)
- New Planet Gluten-Free Beer: Raspberry Ale
- Lakefront Brewery: New Grist
- Glutenberg: India Pale Ale (Montreal based)
- RedBridge
- New Planet Tread Lightly
- Bard's Tale Dragon's Gold

Gluten-Free Hard Ciders:

- Ace Pear Cider
- Angry Orchard
- Blue Mountain Cider Company
- Blackthorn Cider
- Bulmer's Hard Cider
- Crispin Cider
- Gaymer Cider Company
- Harpoon Craft Cider
- J.K Scrumpy's Organic Hard Cider
- Lazy Jack's Cider
- Magner's Cider
- Newton's Folly Hard Cider
- Original Sin Hard Cider
- Smith and Forge Hard Cider
- Spire Mountain Draft Cider
- Strongbow Cider
- Stella Artois Apple and Pear Hard Cider
- Woodchuck
- Woodpeck Cider

Vodka:

- Absolut Vodka
- Unflavored Brandy
- Bombora Vodka
- Boyd and Blair
- Cayman Blue Vodka
- Chopin Polish Vodka
- Ciroc
- Devotion Vodka
- Famous Vodka
- Krome Vodka
- Smirnoff Vodka

Rum:

- Appleton Estate Jamaica Rum
- Bacardi Gold, Superior, 151 and flavored versions
- Bayou Rum
- Bundaberg Rum
- Captain Morgan Rum
- Cruzan Rum
- Mount Gay Rum

Other:

- Cold River Gin
- Harvev's Bristol
- Cream
- Cointreau
- Hennessy Cognac
- Jack Daniel's
- Jaegermeister

Tequila:

Traditionally made tequila comes from the agave plant which is gluten-free. However, there are mixed brands that are cut with other grains to cheapen the quality. Check for "Mixto" on the label and avoid those that have it!

Avoid:

- Jameson Irish Whiskey Johnnie Walker Scotch
- Kahlua
- Bailey's Irish Cream

List of Ingredients to Avoid

- Wheat (and any food such as bread, pastas, tortillas, etc. that are made with wheat)
- Spelt
- Barley (including barley malt)
- Rye
- Wheat Starch
- Seitan
- Triticale and Mir (a cross between wheat and rye)
- Vital Gluten
- Wheatberries
- Durum
- Semolina
- Modified food starch
- Farina
- Self-basting turkey
- Farro
- Pre-packaged seasoning
- Graham
- Processed, packaged food items
- Kamut ®
- Brewer's Yeast
- Emmer
- Some candies (like - Gravy licorice)
- Veggie burgers (unless specified as gluten-free)
- Broth
- Fried Foods
- Soy sauce
- Imitation crab
- Worcestershire sauce meat/fish
- Beer (unless specified as gluten-free)
- Some lunch meats and hot dogs
- Dressings
- Malt
- Sauces
- Matzo
- Ravioli
- Pasta
- Dumplings
- Couscous
- Gnocchi
- Ramen
- Udon
- Soba
- Croissants
- Pita
- Naan
- Bagels
- Flatbread
- Cornbread
- Potato bread
- Muffins
- Donuts
- Rolls
- Cakes
- Cookies
- Pie crusts
- Graham crackers Brownies
- Pretzels Corn flakes/Rice
- puffs Pancakes
- Waffles
- French Toast
- Crepes Biscuits

List of Foods to Avoid (Unless Specifically Marked GF)

- o Granola
- o Panko Breadcrumbs
- o Stuffing
- o Dressing
- o Croutons
- o Cream sauces made with a roux
- o Flour Tortillas
- o Malt beverages

Check These Labels Carefully

- o Energy Bars
- o Granola Bars
- o French fries
- o Potato chips
- o Soup
- o Multi-grain/Artisan chips
- o Marinades
- o Starch/Dextrin
- o Brown rice syrup Eggs served at restaurants
- o Meat Substitutes
- o Cheesecake filling
- o Lipstick/lip gloss/lip balm
- o Communion wafers
- o Herbal or nutritional supplements
- o Over-the-counter drugs
- o Play-dough

Resources to Help You Identify GF Foods, Grocery Items & Restaurants Celiac Resources:

Celiac Central: http://www.celiaccentral.org/support-groups

http://www.celiaccentral.org

Celiac: http://celiac.org

Celiac Support Association: http://www.csaceliacs.org

American Celiac: http://americanceliac.org

Gluten-Free Groups:

Gluten Intolerance Group: https://www.gluten.org

Gluten-Free Media Group: http://www.glutenfreemg.com

Trader Joe's Gluten-Free: http://www.traderjoes.com

Whole Food's Gluten-Free: https://www.wholefoodsmarket.com

Gluten-Free restaurant options:

Olive Garden: http://www.olivegarden.com

Red Lobster: https://www.redlobster.com

BJ's: http://www.bjsrestaurants.com

Chevy's: http://glutenfreeguidehq.com

Mimi's Café: http://glutenfreeinsd.com

It is easier than ever to avoid gluten and I have given you an easy to follow handout to start removing this toxin from your body.

Make sure when you remove gluten you aren't adding in a lot of gluten-free products. Most of these come from a package and are filled with unhealthy, unnatural ingredients.

If it comes in a package and says gluten-free then you should probably skip it and choose a healthier option.

This week we are also going to start with some gentle movement

You don't want you to be over exercising because this will put your adrenal glands out of balance which will send stress signals to the body and stop the signals that it is time to make a baby...

...however, gentle restorative exercise will help your body relax and fill it with endorphins and feel-good chemicals.

Focus on relaxing and incorporating restorative forms of exercise such as yin or restorative yoga. This type of workout regimen will not only lower your cortisol levels, but it will also become a sustainable practice that you can continue to enjoy throughout pregnancy provided your doctor approves.

Some movements I recommend are –

Stretching
Yoga
Tai Chi
Deep breathing
Beginner meditation

Move Your Body

When we think of exercise, so many of us immediately picture trying to run for miles or spending hours at the gym. Let me assure you; you don't need to train for a marathon (unless you want to!) to experience the mental and physical health benefits of movement and exercise. However, if you have any chronic health condition or want to avoid getting one, you must get your body moving. Regular exercise and activity help to support all aspects of physical and mental health. Here are just a few of the incredible health and wellness benefits, including:

- Improves mood, libido, and sleep
- Balances blood sugar and reduces insulin resistance
- Moves the lymph through the body to remove toxicity and boost white blood cells
- Reduces chronic inflammation and the accompanying symptoms
- Stimulates endorphins, metabolic function, and improves neurological and immune health
- Supports cardiovascular health and reduces the risk of diabetes, heart attack, and hypertension

Pretty good reasons to get moving, aren't they? So, what's stopping you from getting up and getting your move on?

The Myths About Exercise

Too many people don't bother exercising or engaging in physical activity because of the limiting beliefs and myths surrounding exercise:

- "No pain, no gain" where you feel you must push yourself so hard every time you work out.
- Exercise takes up too much time.
- It's too expensive to join a gym or buy exercise equipment.
- You don't know what the "right" fitness regimen is.
- Let's look at these a little deeper.

Exercise doesn't have to be a painful, sweat-soaked misery! Yes, if you're trying something new, you may experience a bit of tenderness the next day, but you don't have to push yourself to where you can't get out of bed the next day. Exercise can be a walk, yoga, or riding a bike, or you can start off slowly and work your way up if you decide running, aerobics, or Zumba is your exercise of choice.

Even 15 minutes a day is beneficial! Current medical guidelines recommend 150 minutes of moderate activity or 75 minutes of vigorous activity each week. If you can block out just 15 minutes a day for cardiovascular activity, or 30 minutes a day of steady walking, you're going to see the benefits both mentally and physically. I recommend getting your exercise in earlier in the day. That way you have it done and are less likely to have something come up or be too tired at the end of the day to get in some movement.

Exercise can be free! Don't feel like you need fancy equipment, the best workout clothes, or a gym membership. If you can get outside, walking is one of the best exercises you can do - it's low-impact but still gets the blood moving and the heart pumping. Get a comfortable pair of shoes, and you're set! If you want something a little more exciting, there are plenty of exercise videos on YouTube, or download a free app like Sworkit or Fitbit coach to customize your activity!

There is only one "right" fitness routine: the one you will do consistently! Find what you love and do it regularly!

Getting Started and Staying Motivated

When it comes to getting started, just dive in and start doing it! If you're not sure what type of exercise you like, try some new things out. Find a couple of activities you love – yoga, swimming, walking, spin class, biking, running, Zumba, strength or balance exercises - if it looks like something you're curious about, give it a shot! You'll discover what you enjoy, and if you love it, you're going to stick with it.

Also, some people enjoy exercise as a solitary activity, and some like to engage with a friend or a family member. If you want to use your exercise time as personal time, make it something to look forward to. Use that time to listen to your favorite music or find podcasts that lift you up or energize you, such as Oprah's SuperSoul Conversations or The Daily Boost.

If you like to mix exercise and socializing, recruit a friend or family member to join you. Keep each other accountable, and also have fun. If you don't have anyone able to join you, that's okay! Check for exercise classes and walking groups at local churches or community centers to help find your exercise buddies or look for local groups on Facebook or MeetUp.

Make a Plan to Get Moving

If you want to see what your baseline is for how much exercise you should be getting or where you'd like to be, I recommend getting a pedometer to see how much natural movement you get each day. This can be a real eye-opener! You'd be amazed at how much walking you're doing just in day-to-day activities like housework, chasing after the dog, or doing yard work! Wear your pedometer for a few days to get a baseline. Then try to increase your steps by 10% to 20% each week until you are consistently close to 10,000 steps a day.

Then, create a schedule for yourself. If you do well with structure, make exercise an "appointment" that you keep at certain times during the week. If you like routine, create a daily schedule, and include exercise at a time where you won't bump it off the schedule. Find what works for you!

Don't Get Discouraged

Too many people feel that if they miss one workout or a few days of walking, they may as well quit, or they end up just falling out of the habit very easily. Just take one day at a time. Yes, even if you missed a day, a week, or a month of regular exercising, make today the day you get it back! Every day you exercise, you're doing amazing things for your physical, mental, and emotional health and well-being.

Session #4 Client Action Guide

My action steps for this session are:

a) Add up to 20 grams of protein per meal per day.

b) Add up to 26 grams of fiber per day

c) Start removing gluten from your diet.

d) Adding healthy fats to my diet. 1-3 TBSP with each meal.

e) Begin removing gluten from your diet if you aren't already gluten-free.

What are some action steps that you want to add-

_____
_____
_____
_____
_____
_____
_____

My new favorite recipe for the week is-

_____
_____
_____
_____
_____
_____
_____

NOTES

NOTES

NOTES

NOTES

Client Testimonial   - **Angie and Chris A.**

When this couple came to me, they had been trying for about 6 months and Angie had been recently diagnosed with PCOS. She was so upset and really wanted to believe that she would eventually get pregnant even though her doctor told her the odds were against her.

Kela really helped me get my diet right so I could start losing weight and get my PCOS under control. She helped me to find foods that I loved and that worked with my body. She was there to hold my hand when I needed it and encouraged me through this tough time. After working with her for about 6 months, I couldn't believe it.

I was pregnant!

I couldn't be happier. This is a dream come true. If you have any doubts about working with coach Kela, I want to tell you to just do it! Trust the process, follow the action steps, believe it will happen, and it will. You will get pregnant.

Chapter 6

Intentional Foods and Environmental Factors Puzzle Piece

** This chapter is compatible with **Week 5** of The Hormone Puzzle Online Coaching program. **

(www.hormonepuzzle.com)

Hi friends, welcome back! It's time to start week 5. As always let's start our week with what is going well. What went well last week? Let's write that down in our journal.

Were you able to add in your fat, protein and fiber into each meal? Were you consistent? If not, what happened? How can you course correct for this week?

Write this all down. Get it out of your head and onto paper. Whatever you wrote is perfect.

This week we are going to talk about adding in fermented foods and why that is important as well as talking about detoxing your home and your environment.

Fermented foods are so important because there are many benefits to your health from eating fermented foods, including boosting your fertility.

This is because you are quickly adding millions of beneficial bacteria to your gut which helps our digestive system work at its best and is crucial.

Fermented foods contain large amounts of probiotic microbes that are needed to improve intestinal bacteria and improve digestion.

These natural probiotics help in aiding IBS, boosting immunity, regulating hormones, reducing inflammation and controlling blood sugar levels. Incorporating traditional fermented foods into your diet will promote a healthy gut, which in turn lowers levels of food intolerances and other immune-response diseases, helping you to absorb more of the essential nutrients from the foods you eat and since we know everything starts in the gut, having a healthy gut will increase your fertility and overall health.

Healthy balanced gut bacteria are necessary for processing toxins which lowers inflammation and reduces toxin exposure for the developing fetus.

The reason you want to eat lots of fermented foods is because…

…they have large amounts of probiotic microbes that are needed to improve intestinal bacteria and improve digestion which boosts fertility.

These natural probiotics help in –

- o aiding IBS
- o boosting immunity
- o regulating hormones
- o reducing inflammation
- o controlling blood sugar levels

Incorporating traditional fermented foods into your diet will promote a healthy gut, which in turn lowers levels of food intolerances and other immune-response diseases, helping you to absorb more of the essential nutrients from the foods you eat.

This is very important during pre-conception because remember we are trying to put our bodies into the optimal state for conception, therefore, a happy gut equals a happy body ready to reproduce.

Fermented Foods

When you focus on incorporating fermented foods into your diet, you help to support your immune system by fortifying your gut micro-biome. Healthy, balanced gut bacteria is necessary for processing toxins which lowers inflammation and reduces toxin exposure for the developing fetus.

Here is a list of the most popular fermented foods.

Try eating at least 1 of these per meal –

1. Sauerkraut
2. Kefir
3. Miso
4. Tempeh
5. Yogurt (full-fat)
6. Nano
7. Pickled cucumber
8. Beer
9. Buttermilk
10. Apple Cider
11. Pickles (lactic acid fermented)
12. Raw Cheese

"As I look back on my life, I realize that every time I thought I was being rejected from something good, I was actually being redirected to something better."

- Dr. Steve Maraboli

It is also important to add citrus foods and cruciferous vegetables into your magic plate.

Clinical evidence shows that you can increase progesterone production from the ovary by increasing the intake of Vitamin C rich foods.

The reason we are adding in cruciferous vegetables, is that when you focus on adding in these specific vegetables, they work to flush toxins out of the body, including excess estrogens (make sure to cook them lightly to keep thyroid safe).

Buckwheat, carob, and grapefruit all contain a compound called "Inositol" which reduces androgen levels associated with PCOS (Poly-Cystic Ovarian Syndrome) which can disrupt ovulation and impede a potential pregnancy.

You can also supplement it with Inositol if you aren't getting enough from your diet. See my Fullscript dispensary for the one I recommend.

https://us.fullscript.com/welcome/coachkela

PCOS is the number one cause of ovulatory infertility problems

Sea vegetables (such as Kombu and Kelp) are also great to incorporate into your diet as a nutritional source of Iodine which is important for thyroid function.

Eating specific foods during pre-conception is what I like to call intentional eating.

It isn't just about being healthy but it's about eating specific foods that will work with your body to put it into the optimal state for conception, so you get pregnant naturally.

Now we are going to switch gears and talk about **cutting toxins from your environment** and why this is so important.

Cutting toxins such as beauty products, household cleaners, pesticides, and herbicides will not only protect your body from these natural invaders but will keep you as healthy as possible which is what you want when trying to conceive.

Some known toxins are - (edible and non-edible)

PFOA's- Do not cook on pre-2008 Teflon pans or consume microwave popcorn- both are major sources of perfluorooctanoic acid PFOA, a synthetic chemical that causes increased rates of infertility

Alcohol- Women who consume at least one alcoholic beverage per day have a nearly 50% greater risk of ovulatory infertility than women who drink no alcohol.

Sugar- Sugar is one of the worst things you can put in your body if you are trying to conceive, blood sugar balance and inflammation are two of the leading causes of infertility conditions, PCOS and Endometriosis. Avoid sugar at all costs especially when trying to conceive.

Low and fat-free Dairy- Women who eat lots of low-fat dairy products face an 85% higher risk of ovulatory infertility than women who consume little to no dairy

Trans Fats- consuming a mere 4 grams of trans fat a day about 1 small donut or fast food fried item doubles your risk of ovulatory infertility

Excessive caffeine or soda- these drinks are terrible for you when trying to conceive. The combination of the inflammation and metabolic changes caused by too much blood-sugar-spiking sweeteners and gut-bacteria-changing artificial sweeteners, Avoid soda and excessive caffeine at all costs.

Excessive red meat- The reason you should avoid excessive red meat Some red meats are high in saturated fat, which raises blood cholesterol. High levels of LDL cholesterol increase the risk of heart disease. This makes your body a toxic environment breading disease which is the opposite of what you want when you are trying to conceive.

How to find if your products are toxic –

You should begin removing all these products from your house and lifestyle.

You can go to www.ewg.org/skindeep

The Environmental Working Group is an American activist group that specializes in research and advocacy in the areas of agricultural subsidies, toxic chemicals, drinking water pollutants, and corporate accountability. EWG is a non-profit organization.

On their website, you can look up all your products (to see if they are toxic and if so, find products to replace them). I would start with your food and then work your way to your skincare and make-up and then to your household products.

Don't try to do it all at once or it will be very overwhelming and expensive.

Start small and as you run out of products, then replace them with a cleaner version.

How to find clean products and their importance. Choosing clean products to put on your body and to use in your home is just as important as what you eat. Your skin is your largest organ and what you put on it greatly affects your organs, hormones, and fertility. You also pick up toxins all around you from your household cleaners which can greatly affect and disrupt your endocrine system which is a huge factor in your ability to conceive.

This list will provide you with suggestions on how you can search for clean products for your body and home. I would start by switching one or two out and as you run out of products switch out until all your products are safe for you and your environment.

Use these websites to search for clean products –

http://www.ewg.org

http://www.madhippie.com

http://www.grove.com

Cleaning products –

www.branchbasics.com and www.norwex.com

Beauty products –

www.annmariegianni.com

Great all-natural cleaning product –

baking soda, vinegar, and peroxide.

Glass cleaner –

white vinegar, water, and citrus oil

Dish soap –

castile soap, lavender oil, and tea tree oil

Laundry detergent –

baking soda, washing powder, and shredded castile soap

Dishwashing powder –

baking soda, washing powder, and salt

Deodorant –

¼ cup baking soda, 5 TBSP coconut oil, 10 drops essential oil (lavender or lemon), ¼ cup organic corn starch or arrowroot. Mix and store in an airtight jar.

Dryer sheets –

6 face terry cloth face towels, 1 glass jar, 8 drops of bergamot essential oil, 5 drops lavender essential oil, ¾ cup white vinegar. In a glass measuring cup mix ¾ cup white vinegar with your essential oils. You can use any of them but the two I picked above worked very well. Pour a little bit of the vinegar/essential oil mixture in the bottom of the glass jar then add 2 cloths on top. Repeat until all the liquid is used. Turn the jar upside down a few times and then let sit for 24 hours. When ready to use take 1 cloth and put with wet clothes. If it is soaking wet wring it out a little. You want it damp. Once used you can put back in the jar and re-saturate it to make damp again.

All-purpose cleaner –

1½ cups distilled water, ½ cup white cleaning vinegar, 1 tsp castile soap, 20-40 drops essential oil (I like lemon and orange). Combine the water, white vinegar, and essential oils in a clean empty glass spray bottle. Shake gently to combine ingredients and use on any non-porous surface in your home.

Body lotion –

⅓ cup coconut oil, ⅓ cup shea butter, 10 drops lavender essential oil, 5 drops chamomile essential oil (optional) and a mason jar. Place shea butter in the microwave to soften, mix in your room temperature coconut oil with hand or stand mixer for 15 minutes until light and fluffy, now mix in your essential oils and transfer to a mason jar.

Body wash –

1 cup castile soap, ⅔ cup honey ¼ cup extra virgin olive oil and 1 tsp vitamin E oil. Combine all ingredients into a reusable bottle and mix.

You can search for any product you want on www.pinterest.com. Search DIY and all-natural and start switching out your products today. The environment, your skin, and your wallet will thank you.

"You may have to fight a battle more than once to win it."

- Margaret Thatcher

Now let's switch gears and talk about why it is so important to buy organic. Have you heard the saying you are what you eat? Well, I am going to take that one step further and say…

…you are what you eat, eats.

That means that when you eat an animal you also eat whatever they eat. Meaning if you are trying to eat clean, remove toxins and are struggling with infertility and you eat non-organic meat or vegetables/fruit then you are eating corn/soy from what the animal ate, you are eating pesticides/herbicides from fruits and vegetables.

Why would you do all this work to just sabotage your efforts?

It's not just as simple as washing the food especially for fruits and vegetables, because the toxic chemicals are in the soil and grow into the food. You must buy organic to avoid these chemicals and truly eat clean.

I know it can be overwhelming. I know what your thinking, coach Kela I can't afford to eat all organic. I would go broke. It is actually more affordable than you think and because organic food tastes so much better you will be satisfied easier and quicker than eating non-organic counterparts.

My advice is to start small.

When doing your shopping, look for organic items on sale. Many stores will offer in-season foods at a discount. You can also visit your local farmers' market. They always have a great selection of in-season fruits and vegetables. Local farmers also frequent these events. Get to know them.

What better way to get clean meat, than to buy direct from the farmers?

You will also want to be mindful of your fish sources. Buying sustainable, deep water, wild-caught fish and not farmed is what is most important when choosing fish. Buying fish with these parameters will not only have your fish tasting better but will have way more vitamins and nutrients than their farmed brothers and sisters.

If you can't find anything on sale and you still want to start implementing organic fruits and vegetables into your diet choose ones on the **dirty dozen** list that I have included here.

Dirty Dozen & Clean 15

The Environmental Working Group (EWG) evaluates fruits and vegetables to determine their overall pesticide exposure. The Dirty Dozen and Clean 15 help consumers prioritize which foods are most important to purchase organic when trying to limit pesticide exposure.

The lists are determined by evaluating six factors and scoring each item. The dirty dozen are the 12 fruits and vegetables with the highest pesticide loads. The Clean 15 are the fruits and vegetables with the least pesticide residue.

Recently, the EWG has added a "plus" category to their dirty dozen to include select foods that contain trace amounts of highly hazardous pesticides. They don't meet the traditional standards to be included in the list, yet are included as a plus due to insecticide contamination.

Clean 15: Doesn't Need to be Organic

1. Asparagus
2. Avocados
3. Cabbage
4. Cantaloupe
5. Cauliflower
6. Eggplant
7. Grapefruit
8. Kiwi
9. Mangoes
10. Onions
11. Papayas
12. Pineapples
13. Sweet corn
14. Sweet peas (frozen)
15. Sweet potatoes

Dirty Dozen: Always Choose Organic

1. Apples
2. Celery
3. Cherry tomatoes
4. Cucumbers
5. Grapes
6. Nectarines
7. Peaches
8. Potatoes
9. Snap peas
10. Spinach
11. Strawberries
12. Sweet bell peppers
+ hot peppers
+ kale/collard greens

Should you eat organic? – Yes, fruits and veggies that are certified organic can't be treated with any pesticides, herbicides, heavy metals or something called slug which is basically this chemical make up of junk that I don't want to be ingesting. Pay now or pay later.

Organic tastes better and has more vitamins and nutrients than non-organic. Study after study has shown that organic veggies have WAY more nutrients than non-organic Same for organic meats. Organic meat dines on mostly grass producing a healthier tastier fatty-acid profile.

I wish there were more studies like this but big food, big ag, biotech companies that don't produce organic food but have deep pockets pay to have these studies never done or never published.

Better for the waistline – Organic foods are free from antibiotics, growth hormones, pesticides and synthetic preservatives. These are all endocrine-disrupting chemicals that promote weight gain, hormone disruption and infertility. Minimizing your exposure to these will help you lose weight and keep it off

Easier to eat cleaner ingredients – when you eat all organic it helps you avoid highly processed toxic foods. Eating certified organic helps you stay away from many food additives

Protect your family from harmful pesticides – Avoid a cocktail of synthetic chemicals including roundup. Even when you wash your food when it is grown in soil with these pesticides, it's in the food not just on the outside of it so you can't wash it off. Ingesting these chemicals can cause all sorts of things from cancer, Alzheimer's, Parkinson's, type 2 diabetes, obesity, food allergies, hormone imbalance and infertility.

These are just a few reasons to buy 100% certified organic all the time but if you can't and it's just not in the budget especially buy the dirty dozen.

The dirty dozen is a list created by the environmental working group. These are fruits and vegetables with the least toxins. If you can't shop 100% organic at least buy the items on the dirty dozen list. These are the ones with the most toxins on them. Think of it like this.

If you eat the skin then you want organic, if not then you can buy non-organic.

I, of course, want you buying all organic but if you can't afford it or if that is too big of a task then start small and start with the dirty dozen list.

The next thing you will want to do is to start removing anything that is a toxin in your environment. This includes beauty products- parabens, environmental chemicals, toxic foods, toxic thoughts, etc.

Start small and remove one item at a time until you are 100% toxin-free.

Well, we have come to the end of another week. I am so proud of you. You have changed so much in these last 4 weeks and I couldn't be more excited for you and this new journey you are on. Keep up the great work. Make sure to do your action guide with the action steps. This will be the difference in the results you want or not.

Let's end this week with an aha or appreciation about what you learned. Write down the one thing you learned or took away from this week. No matter how big or how small, a win is a win!

You got this girl.

Week 5 Client Action Guide

1. Which foods are you going to switch out this week for organic-

_____
_____
_____

2. Add in three fermented foods to your diet. List those three here-

_____
_____
_____

3. These are the toxic products I am removing from my environment-

_____
_____
_____

4. These are the replacements for those products-

_____
_____
_____

NOTES

NOTES

NOTES

NOTES

Client Testimonial   - **Katie and Chris S.**

When Katie found me, she had been living with PCOS but didn't know it for many, many years. Once she found out, she took important steps to prepare her body for a healthy pregnancy.

It took her well over a decade to figure out that she has PCOS. No doctor was ever able to point it out. She didn't menstruate regularly and so she started researching PCOS online before she was even ready to have children just to try to figure out her body. She came across me and the work that I do, and it really hit home that she can do this naturally and so she jumped in with both feet and her and her husband began working with me.

> **"I don't think I would have my incredible son without Coach Kela's help".**

She took my advice to use natural progesterone cream to combat PCOS. It worked wonders and quickly got her cycle going and made her feel better in general. After about 6 weeks of this and changing a few other things in her diet she was finally able to report that…

> **…She was pregnant!**

She and Chris couldn't believe it. She knew that without finding me and doing my protocol, she and her husband could have stayed in victim mode and let PCOS determine their destiny. They chose to fight and won.

Chapter 7

Basal Body Temperature and Meal Timing Piece

*This chapter is compatible with **Week 6** of The Hormone Puzzle Online Coaching program. *

(www.hormonepuzzle.com)

Hey friend! How did your week go? What went well last week? Let's celebrate our wins by writing them down in our journal. Were you able to start removing toxins from your environment? Were you able to add in your fermented foods? Were you consistent? If not, what happened? How can you course-correct for next week? Write this all down. Get it out of your head and on paper. Thank you for sharing that.

This week we are going to be talking about **basal body temperature** and the importance of **meal timing** and **mentally prepping for fertility**.

When you eat is just as important as what you eat.

Timing your meals properly is going to help your food work with your body instead of against it. You are in charge of your fertility so let's use your meals to push you towards fertility instead of working against.

One mantra you will want to remember when it comes to meal timing is,

Eat like a queen at breakfast, a king at lunch, a pauper at dinner.

This means that your biggest meal should be at lunch and your dinner should be a supplementation meal and fairly small. You will want to eat within an hour of waking to get your metabolism rocking. I know there are different schools of thought on this one, however, through all my research and personal experience eating within an hour of waking works for most clients. However, some people do better on a longer fast.

If you stop eating around 7 pm then you won't want to eat anything again until at least 7 the next morning.

Some people stretch that to 9 so it's 12-14 hours between their last meal and their first. Play with this window and see what works for you. Listen to your internal hunger speedometer and determine when you should eat your first meal.

Eat within an hour of waking to get your metabolism rockin'.

Speaking of your hunger speedometer, at each meal, check-in with your Hunger Speedometer.

Practice eating until 80% full

Notice when you naturally get hungry again after eating until 80% full. Is it 2 hours? 3? 4? Measure, when you get hungry again, where on the Hunger Speedometer are you? (in other words, are you hungry enough for another meal or a snack?) This process will help you discover how many meals and snacks are right for YOU.

"It always seems impossible until it's done."

- Nelson Mandela

Fueling your body when it needs it and not when it doesn't will keep your blood sugar steady which will help with PCOS as well as keep you satiated.

Mealtimes will likely be about 4-5 hours apart for most people.

The more active someone is, the more frequently they may need to eat.

Focus on Magic Plate meals for proper macronutrient balance at each meal.

Eat "Magic Snacks" between meals (includes fiber, fat, and protein with every snack).

Now let's switch gears a little and talk about something I like to call the…

20 Minute Meal

This is a fun little game you can play with yourself to make sure you are getting the most out of your meals.

This practice lets your body enjoy the experience of eating which helps you to eat with all your senses and treat your meals as an experience and not just another thing that you have to do.

Eating each meal for at least 20 minutes gives your body time to recognize it has had an actual meal and therefore is able to use all the vitamins and nutrients you just ingested as well as it gives your stomach time to send signals to your brain that you are actually done and your body will stop searching for food.

In the beginning it will be difficult to make it to 20 minutes but trust me you will get there. The way this game works is, I want you to pick a meal, any meal you want and eat normally. Set a timer and when finished see how long it took you to eat that meal.

Most people are shocked to see how quickly they eat.

I think the first time I played this game my meal took about 3 minutes.

20-Minute Meal Journal

Use this handy journal to keep track of your 20-Minute Meal Method experience.

How to Do the 20-Minute Meal

Starting with your next meal, follow these simple steps.

Step #1:

- Check the clock before you start your next meal
- Eat your meal at the pace you normally would
- Check the clock at the end of your meal
- Jot down how much time your entire meal took in your 20-Min Meal Journal

Bonus Tip:

No judgment here. The 20-Min Meal Journal is NOT a food journal. It's NOT about being "bad" or "good". It's about discovering if you're taking enough time during your meals for your tummy to tell you what the right amount of food is for your body. The first time I did this, my meal lasted 3 whole minutes.

I repeat, no judgment.

Step #2:

- At your next meal, increase your mealtime by 5 minutes more than your last time
- Document your mealtime, when you started to feel full, your mood and your "aha!" moments in your 20-Min Meal Journal

Step #3:

- Keep repeating Step #2 with each meal until meals last at least 20 minutes
- Document each day in your 20-Min Meal Journal

Step #4:

- o Note at what time during the 20-Minute Meal that you feel **satisfied** and when you tip over to **full** in your 20-Min Meal Journal

Step #5:

- o Make each meal for the next 7 days a 20-Minute Meal (or longer!)
- o Note in your 20-Min Meal Journal if you feel uncomfortably full on the **20-Minute Meal Journal.**

TYPE A PERSONALITY ALERT:

Don't worry about filling in this journal "perfectly" or "right".

Relax and let yourself have fun with this…

You will be surprised and delighted at what you discover!

Day	Meal Minutes	I Felt Satisfied At __ Minutes	My Mood Today	My "Aha!" Moment Today
SAMPLE				
Day One	3	------------	Anxious!	Wow, I get super stressed about whether or not I'm being "good" or "bad".
Day Two	8	Couldn't tell	Annoyed	I've gotten so cynical…I think I believe that nothing is going to work for me. ;-(
Day Three	13	I think 13?	Curious	Felt really relaxed today during meals….and peeing like crazy! I think when my body relaxes it starts releasing weight. Cool!

Day	Meal Minutes	I Felt Satisfied At __ Minutes	My Mood Today	My "Aha!" Moment Today
Day One		------------		
Day Two				
Day Three				
Day Four				
Day Five				
Day Six				
Day Seven				

YOUR TURN

Now that you know the 20-Minute Meal process, let's look at the different ways you can use it in your day-to-day life. This will help you lose weight and actually ENJOY it!

Using the 20-Minute Meal Method in your day to day life is super simple because:

- No one will know you're doing it (love that!)
- You don't have to miss out on parties or dinners with friends or sweethearts.
- You don't have to postpone your vacation or travel to accommodate a "diet".
- You don't have to restrict the kinds of foods you eat.

All you need to use the 20-Minute Meal every day is…

1. A clock or a timer somewhere in sight

2. A pen, a tablet, computer or smartphone

3. Your 20-Minute Meal Journal

   a) Make a copy of the journal in this book or create your own on a smart phone, tablet or computer.

   b) The 20-Minute Meal Journal only takes 90 seconds a day to complete, and you'll get **even more powerful results** if you commit to completing it every day for the next 7 days.

- Keep times meal consistent (at least during the workweek).

  For example, every day breakfast is at 9, lunch is at 12:30, dinner is at 6

- Try to eat most dinners before 7 pm or 7:30 pm in a given week (or at least 2 hours before bed).
- Observe the effect of caffeine on blood sugar.
- Caffeine masks natural rhythm by providing a "fake" source of energy.
- Letting go of or decreasing caffeine can help you reclaim your most powerful metabolism.
- If you have mood swings and energy dips, exploring your relationship with caffeine could be a key to resolving those issues.
- That doesn't mean never having caffeine again, it does mean experimenting with the amount you drink until you discover your "true energy" (i.e. how you feel without "fake" energy).

Once you know that, then you can choose when and if you drink caffeine, instead of needing to drink it compulsively or habitually.

Now let's Talk about prepping for fertility and getting pregnant.

Are you mentally prepared for this?

Are you ready to be a mom?

Is your spouse or partner ready to be a parent?

What might you have to let go of in order to become pregnant?

What new perspective can you adopt?

We will talk about stress next week. Explore how you feel about being pregnant. What comes up for you? What does it mean to you to be pregnant? Who is influencing your desire to be a mom? Who are your material influences- are your associations positive or negative? If you are feeling pressure around getting pregnant- where is that pressure coming from (society, spouse, parents, etc.)?

Getting mentally prepared for pregnancy is just as important as getting physically prepared.

We always hear about what to eat, what vitamins to take and what exercises to do but what about our mental health? Studies have shown that mental and emotional well-being during pre-conception and pregnancy can have an impact on birth outcomes as well as mental states during the postpartum period.

Some steps you can take to help mentally prepare yourself for pregnancy is taking time for –

- Self-care
- Deep breathing
- Meditation
- Talk to your partner
- Banish negative self talk
- Lean on family and friends
- Join other expecting couples' groups

Now let's talk about **basal body temperature charting**. Your BBT is your temperature when you are at complete rest. Your basal body temperature changes based on the number of factors, including your hormones.

When you ovulate, the hormone progesterone causes your temperature to rise. It remains higher throughout the two-week wait. Then, just before your period starts, the hormone progesterone drops. This means your basal body temperature will drop too unless you are pregnant, in which case your temperature will remain higher because progesterone will stay high.

To find out what your basal body temperature is, you must take it in the morning before you get out of bed or move around. Don't go to the bathroom first or do anything. Any activity AT ALL will cause your temperature to rise and your reading will be off.

It is essential that you take your temperature correctly, otherwise your temperature will not be accurate, and you may not be able to detect ovulation.

Use the chart I have provided in this book or create your own to record your temperature each morning

Basal Body Temperature and Cervical Mucus Chart

Dates Covered:_____   **Cycle Number:** _____

Cycle Day	1	2	3	4	5	6	7	8	9	10	11	12	13	14	15	16	17	18	19	20	21	22	23	24	25	26	27	28	29	30	31	32	33	34	35	36	37	38	39	40
Date																																								
Day of Week																																								
Time																																								
99.0																																								
98.9																																								
98.8																																								
98.7																																								
98.6																																								
98.5																																								
98.4																																								
98.3																																								
98.2																																								
98.1																																								
98.0																																								
97.9																																								
97.8																																								
97.7																																								
97.6																																								
97.5																																								
97.4																																								
97.3																																								
97.2																																								
97.1																																								
97.0																																								
CM																																								
Sex																																								

Basal Body Temperature (°F) (vertical axis label)

Everything comes to you at the right moment, be patient and trust the universe.

There are a few rules you must follow when taking your BBT-

1. You must take it at the same time every morning (plus or minus no more than 30 minutes).

2. Do not get up, sit up, walk around or go to the bathroom first. The minute you wake up pop the thermometer in your mouth. I know this is so romantic but it's imperative for this to work.

3. You need to have at least 3-4 hours of solid sleep before you take your temperature. If you stayed up all night, or you woke up and walked around in the middle of the night, do not test because your results will be off.

4. You need to use the same thermometer throughout the cycle. If you must buy a new one, then start using it on the first day of your next cycle.

When should you start charting –

Ideally, it should be on the first day of your period and continue to take your BBT every morning throughout your entire cycle.

Every day, mark your waking basal body temperature, along with the time that you took your temperature.

After you have experience with charting, you may discover that you can skip the first few days of your period and start taking your temperature around day 5 or 6. Until you know when you tend to ovulate, though it's best to take your temperature all the way through the cycle.

How do I know when I'm ovulating? Most of my clients prefer using an app such as -

- *o* *Clue Period Tracker, Ovulation*
- *o* *Flo Period & Ovulation Tracker*
- *o* *Glow Cycle & Fertility Tracker.*
- *o* *Fertility Friend FF App*

With these apps you can log a ton of information and reduce your chances of error. Most of these apps will automatically notify you when ovulation likely occurred. If you try taking your temperature yourself, you might worry about making a mistake.

Once you have picked how you want to chart your temperature, it's time to start taking your basal body temperature.

How do I choose my thermometer? There are many thermometers made especially for tracking BBT, but you might not need one. Ideally, you need one that is accurate to 1/10th (98.6) of a degree if you measure in Fahrenheit or 1/100th (37.00) of a degree Celsius.

While many have interesting features, the truth of the matter is, any good, regular ole thermometer will work.

How to read your graph –

Your temperature may rise and fall as your cycle progresses, but you should notice a biphasic pattern after ovulation. This means that before ovulation, the temperatures are on average lower than they are after ovulation.

After you see at least three higher- than - average temperatures in a row, you can most likely say that ovulation occurred on the day before the first high temperature.

If you have been tracking your cervical mucus, then you can be even more sure ovulation occurred on the day before if you noticed fertile cervical mucus in the days leading up to the temperature rise.

If you are lucky, you may notice a sharp dip in temperature on the day of ovulation. Not every woman gets this nice heads-up. If you do notice a consistent dip in temp before the rise from month to month, you should be sure to have sexy time with your partner on that day.

How do I use BBT as part of my fertility treatment and to get pregnant? The main way to use a BBT chart to get pregnant is to look for patterns. Are there certain days in your cycle that you tend to ovulate? You will want to use this information to time your sexual relations better.

For example, if over a three-month period you note that ovulation occurred on days 11, 12 and 15, then on your next cycle, you probably want to time sex between days 6 through 16, with special attention to days 11 through 15.

You don't need to have sex on the day of ovulation to get pregnant. If you have sex just a few times during those days before ovulation, that should be enough to get the sperm to the egg in time. Some couples try to have sex every other day the week before they expect to ovulate. This can sometimes work.

Whether you decide to track your basal temperature or not this is just one more piece in your hormone puzzle which you can choose to do or not.

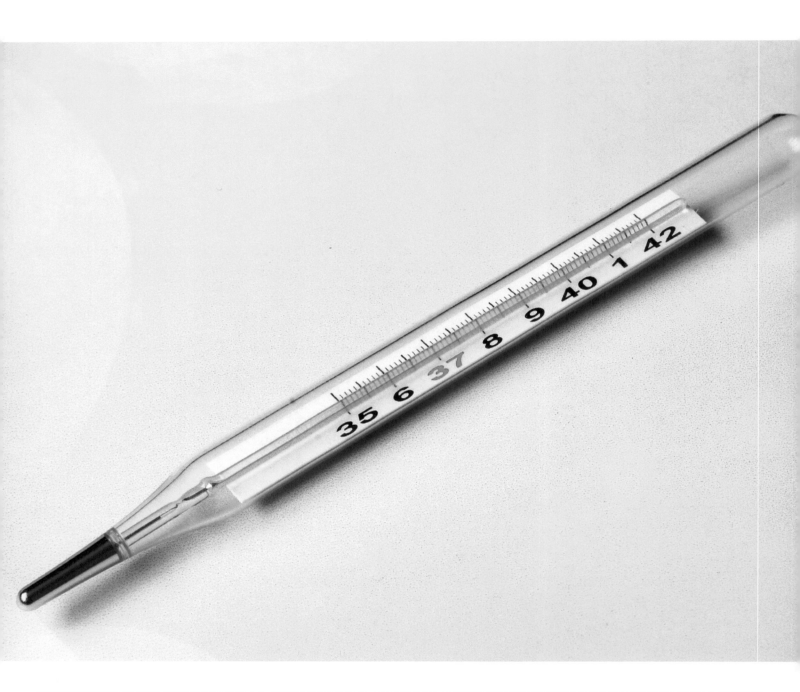

Your empowered action steps for the week are –

Practice meal timing and the 20 Minute Meal.

Start emotionally preparing for pregnancy and to be a mom.

When your cycle starts, begin tracking your BBT, if you so choose.

Client Action Guide - Week 6

What went well-

_____

_____

_____

What toxins did you remove-

_____

_____

_____

What fermented foods did you try-

_____

_____

_____

Use the 20-Minute Meal handout to start slowing your meals down. How long did your last meal take-

_____

_____

_____

Are you mentally prepared for this-

_____
_____
_____

Are you ready to be a mom-

_____
_____
_____

Is your spouse or partner ready to be a parent?

_____
_____
_____

What might you have to let go of in order to release the block you have and become pregnant-

_____
_____
_____

What new perspective must you adopt about becoming pregnant so you can release the stress around it all-

_____
_____
_____

As we close this week, what were your aha's and appreciations about this week. What was one thing you learned or are excited about as you move through this week and into the next?   Write it down in your journal.

Practicing gratitude weekly will boost your morale and make moving forward easier and with the right mindset.

NOTES

NOTES

NOTES

When I met Jennifer and her husband, she was going from doctor to doctor only for them to tell her that all her tests came back normal and there was nothing wrong with her. She was not having a period at all and knew that there was no way that was normal. The doctor's solution was always to put her on birth control.

"After so much time, I gave up on them and I began to do my own research online which is when I ran across coach Kela. I really liked what I saw, however, I was hesitant about ordering anything. I was afraid I wouldn't know how to use her services, or it would be too hard and overwhelming.

After some time of no progress, I decided to give it a try. I purchased her online program which was 8 weeks long and included a fertility cleanse and it was towards the end of the process that I got my period back after two years of nothing!

I gave myself some time before I decided to now try something to help make sure I was ovulating so I could conceive. I decided on a few of her recommended supplements. I also made some major changes in my diet. I was eating as clean as I possibly could, and I was drinking my recommended water intake.

After a few months of everything working the way it was supposed to, I am happy to report...

...I got pregnant and have a beautiful baby daughter

If it wasn't for Coach Kela and her program, I know I would have never had the baby I desired. If I can do it, anyone can. I urge you, do not wait. Hire Kela and start making these changes today. It will be the best decision of your life."

Chapter 8

Stress Puzzle Piece

*This chapter is compatible with **Week 6** of The Hormone Puzzle Online Coaching program. *

(www.hormonepuzzle.com)

Hey lovely! How is your week going? What went well last week? I hope you were able to start honoring your hunger and fullness, implementing the 20-Minute Meal and meal timing, start getting emotionally ready for this next chapter in life and started taking your basal body temperature and charting the findings. Make sure to continue writing it all down in your journal. Remember this is your currency and fuel that will keep you moving forward with ease and excitement.

This week we are going to start talking about…

How to cut stress from your life and how that affects your fertility.

When your body is constantly in a stressed state, you start to make cortisol which is a poison to your body. When your body is in a constant stressed state it shuts down all processes including the signals that it is time to produce a baby. It shuts down digestion, brain function, your immune system is compromised and more. Living in a state of constant stress is the opposite of what you want to do to conceive a healthy baby.

The other piece of this is that your body can determine what is perceived stress and what is actual stress so whether you are being chased by a lion or your boss is yelling at you or you are worried about not being able to conceive, it is all stress to your body.

Define the major sources of stress in your life.

Make a point of quietly reflecting on what the stressors currently are in your life.

What can you change and delegate to make things easier and less stressful? And for the challenges that can't be addressed immediately – where can you shift your perspective? Stress has an inflammatory effect on the body- a woman who desires to conceive needs to proactively work on lowering her stress- response in order to enhance her fertility.

What changes can you make starting today to begin to actively lower your stress levels and begin to enjoy your life on a deeper level?

Being happier and more relaxed, overall, boosts your fertility levels and your chance for conception.

These are all the things that happen when your body is in a constant state of stress.

- **Increased swallowing rate**: A fast swallowing rate is a likely factor in digestive upset.
- **Increased food sensitivities and allergies:** Plenty of anecdotal evidence, most likely due to decreased immunity and leaky gut.
- **Increased cortisol production**: Associated with weight gain (especially in the belly), inability to lose weight or gain muscle, premature aging, unable to conceive.
- **Decreased gut flora populations:** Healthy intestinal bacteria are destroyed by stress, which can lead to immune problems, skin disorders, nutrient deficiencies, digestive distress and inability to conceive and carry a baby to term.
- **Decreased nutrient absorption**: Due to decreased enzymatic production from the stomach, pancreas, and liver, decreased bile flow from the gallbladder, decreased oxygenation and gastrointestinal blood flow.
- **Increase in salt retention:** Can lead to high blood pressure which is terrible for conception.
- **Decrease in thermic efficiency**: Your ability to burn calories is diminished.
- **Decrease in thyroid hormone:** Can lead to a decrease in metabolic activity throughout the body.
- **Increased nutrient excretion:** Urinary loss of calcium, magnesium, potassium, zinc, chromium, selenium, and various microminerals.
- **Increase in blood cholesterol:** Stress by itself will raise LDL levels.
- **Increase in blood platelet aggregation:** A major risk factor in heart disease.
- **Increase in gastric emptying time:** Can lead to constipation; also, a risk factor in diseases of the colon.
- **Decrease in sex hormones:** Can mean lower sex drive, low energy, decreased muscle mass. Which, news flash, you must have sex to get pregnant.
- **Increase in inflammation:** The basis of many significant ailments, including brain and heart disease, which can greatly hinder the ability to conceive.
- **Decrease in gastric emptying time:** Can lead to diarrhea and larger food particles prematurely entering the small intestines, a probable factor in food allergies, sensitivities, and various disease conditions.

To overcome stress and move into a calmer and more centered person which is open and ready to conceive, I recommend gentle meditations and mindful breathing. Please see the gentle, guided meditation on the next page.

Beginners Guide to Meditation

The practice of meditation is a great way to relieve stress, but it also has so many more benefits, from reducing anxiety, depression, eating disorders, emotional eating, addiction, habit change and more. So, what does meditation do? Meditation is now being recommended by doctors everywhere to help in all these areas including over-all health and disease prevention and management of symptoms.

Once you build your basics of meditation and have momentum from consistent practice, you will begin to experience the benefits of more multi-dimensional awareness. This means awareness of who you are in the subtle dimensions which go beyond your physical body, your mind and your emotions. Human beings are multi-dimensional forms of consciousness, and it is in our subtle dimensions that we progressively experience more truthful states of being. It is within our subtle dimensions that we have a true perception of reality.

Meditation and How it Works -

Meditation is a balancing technique. When balance increases, our awareness expands, and all the benefits of meditation begin to unfold. There are many experiences of intense focus that produce meditative states and some examples are: a mother cradling her child and flowing loving feelings or an athlete focusing with precision on the task at hand. The difference is that, when you meditate, it's an internal focus as opposed to an external focus. When we sit, we close our eyes and focus within. We eliminate external distractions and focus on our internal experience.

Most of us live a crazy modern lifestyle with a focus on the objective or external world. The result is that we miss our inner experience which is happening simultaneously. Meditation, with it's internal focus, helps us to emphasize the inner, subjective polarity of our experience. A consistent meditation practice, then, helps create balance between our external and internal experience.

With greater balance through meditation, we can expand our awareness and be more present in the moment to whatever is happening in our lives.

1. First, find a comfortable place where you can sit without distractions for at least 15 minutes.

2. Sit comfortably with your back upright and without back support, if physically possible.

3. Close your eyes and focus within.

4. Focus your attention.
    a. You can focus your attention on your breath and breathing. Breathe in and out. Just watch the movement of your in and out breaths.
    b. You can repeat an affirmation (a positive statement about yourself and life). My favorites are, I am enough, I am powerful, I am capable of anything, God, allow me to work your purpose.
    c. If you use an affirmation, try to feel what it means to you.
    d. You can focus on your heartbeat.
    e. You can use any other method with which you feel comfortable.

5. If you notice your mind thinking, that's okay, just bring your focus back to your technique.

6. When you have completed meditating, it is a good idea to give yourself a few minutes to acclimate slowly back into the activities of your day.

1. The most important advice is to meditate regularly, which means daily. The commitment to a regular, daily practice is more important than any method or technique. Schedule time to meditate in your daily schedule so that it becomes an important appointment with yourself.

2. If you are a beginner meditator, even 15 minutes daily is enough to start.

3. Meditation soundtracks are created in 30-minute segments so that you can meditate for 30–60 minutes in a single session. If you can meditate more than once a day, even better.

4. Brief balancing exercises are also beneficial and are a way to maintain your balance throughout the day.

5. Make sure you choose a time of day that you will not be disturbed. Most people choose early in the morning or late at night. But it really does not matter when you meditate, as long as you can devote a period of time to your practice without being disturbed. Each of us has a unique biorhythm and we know what times are likely to be best for us.

6. If possible, create a space where you can practice your meditation and which you use for nothing else. This could be a spare room or a section of a room.

7. It is also best to meditate at the same time every day.

These tips will assist you in generating momentum. Treat your meditation as a sacred act because it is! If you revere it, the results will be even more impressive.

Meditation generates a lot of power from within. This power, in turn, affects the world around you. So be wakeful and watch the magic and miracles unfold.

More Meditation Tips on How to Meditate Effectively –

1. Affirmations are a modern version of what are termed "mantras" in the East. They are truthful, positive statements that are very effective if you allow the flow positive feelings while you use them. If you are just repeating them unconsciously, however, not much will change. When you simultaneously feel what you are affirming, you bring the experience of your affirmation into your experience in the moment, and with consistent practice, effortlessly into your life.

2. Flowing positive feelings both in meditation and throughout your day is very important. This is just as important as meditating, and it has a powerful impact on the world around you.

3. As you progress in your practice, you will find it becomes completely natural and effortless. When this happens, you can simply drop your technique. However, every meditator knows that the mind becomes active again from time to time and, when it does so, you can resume your technique. So, keep the techniques for quieting the mind ready, and be prepared to use them as needed.

My Mind Won't Stop Thinking – I Can't Meditate

Over the years we have heard it said over and over again: "I can't meditate." When we ask why, the person usually replies, "My mind won't stop. I just keep thinking. So, I don't do it."

Let's clear this confusion up once and for all—your mind does not need to stop thinking to meditate. Your mind is designed to think, so... let it think!

Then, you ask, "What is all this talk about quieting the mind and not thinking?" The basic point is that meditation is about balance, wakefulness and awareness. It is not about forcing something to be a certain way. The restless, unconscious, repetitive mind is a habit. And habits can be changed or broken.

Meditation is about being wakefully present and aware of "what is" happening. If the mind is happening, then be aware of it. Also, because it is habitual, one can direct it from its usual life-negative focus to a life positive focus through affirmations and thus create balance and wakefulness.

Thinking represents the negative, external, objective polarity. Stillness of mind is the positive, internal, subjective polarity. You can't have one polarity without its opposite, so you can't have thinking without stillness and vice versa. Both exist within us at all times.

Meditation increases balance through focus on the non-dominant positive polarity, the internal stillness. This, in turn, expands holistic awareness of both the subjective and objective.

I am serious about the benefits of meditation, I highly suggest "Balance Breaks" throughout your day. Whenever you can remember, take a few minutes to close your eyes and re-balance yourself, reconnect to the energy you generated in your last meditation. Flow positive feelings. Do your 557 breathing.

If you do this a few times a day, the benefits will become more constant throughout your daily life. You will find yourself more consistently present and balanced, no matter what is happening in your world. The importance of this practice cannot be overstated. Use it as frequently as you remember. It's also a great way to maintain balance, whether you are at home or at work. These breaks increase your balance, your effectiveness and your performance.

These balance breaks also can be used when you feel the urge to eat when you are not truly hungry. Whenever that feeling strikes and it isn't time for a meal or snack, take a balance break, practice your 557 breathing and ask yourself, am I hungry for food or something else. Am I bored, tired, anxious, depressed, lonely, stressed...?

Top meditation apps –

- o Headspace
- o Calm
- o Stop, breath, think
- o Smiling mind, mindfulness

Let's switch gears and talk about how,

Breathing exercises increase your ability to manage stress...

...and help to trick your central nervous system into thinking you are calm and relaxed when you might be anxious about not being able to conceive, nervous about childbirth, scared of labor, depressed by the entire situation, whatever you are feeling know that it is ok and normal. This breathing exercise will allow you to slow down for a minute and make you think you are calm and relaxed when you might be feeling one or all those emotions.

The breathing exercise I want you to incorporate into your life is called **box breathing** and this is done in 4 parts hence the name box. You can do this anywhere, anytime and with anyone. You can do it as many or as few times as you need to slow everything down and to trick your central nervous system into thinking you are calm and relaxed when you might be anxious, worried, or STRESSED.

Quick start to 557/Balance Breathing-

I talk about 557/balance breathing in this chapter. How you do this is

Breathe in through your nose for a count of 5
Hold for a count of 5
Out through the mouth for a count of 7
Really pronounce the exhale and make a whooshing sound.

Practicing this breathing will help to trick your central nervous system into thinking you are calm and relaxed when you might be anxious, nervous, excited, stressed, depressed, etc.

Whatever you are feeling, this will slow it all down and allow you to focus and be present. Try it today. I promise you will feel relaxed and renewed in no time.

Breathing Exercise #2 – *Box Breathing* –

The way it works is you will sit in your chair with your spine elongated, (we want to get lots of air into our lungs) feet flat on the floor so that you ground yourself into the earth (if you can do this outside on the grass or sand, even better), eyes closed-

Breathe out through your mouth for a count of 4

In through the nose for a count of 4

Hold for a count of 4

Out through the mouth for another count of 4.

We are going to do it a few times together. Are you ready to try it? Ok. Out through the mouth for a count of 4, 3, 2, 1, in through nose 1, 2, 3, 4, hold 1, 2, 3, 4 and out through the mouth for a count of 4, 3, 2, 1. Great. Keep practicing this daily. Do this when you feel yourself starting to become stressed or whatever emotion you are feeling. Allow this breath to fill you will joy and life and use it to motivate you to keep pushing forward.

Start to journal how you feel about being pregnant after you do your breathing when your mind is open.

Now let's talk about **self-care** and how you can start to add in more and more into your routine and start to make it a habit. Self-care is SO important when trying to conceive. What does self-care look like to you?

- *a bubble bath*
- *a walk with your dog*
- *a massage*
- *getting your nails and toes manicure*

Whatever makes you happy and is focused 100% on you then make sure you are doing that daily.

Put it in your schedule and treat it as a sacred appointment with yourself.

Self-care should not look like folding laundry, doing the dishes or scrolling on IG. It should be something 100% dedicated to you and what you are needing at that moment. Something you love and that will fulfill you.

Personal Nourishment Menu

Here are some of my favorite self-care practices.

Choose one of these to do daily, or make your own list:

- Massage
- Yoga
- Dance
- Sensual pleasure
- Shower
- Green drink
- Facial
- Flowers
- House cleaner
- Mani/Pedi
- Long walk
- Coffee with a friend
- A good book
- A quiet patio
- Sleeping in past 9
- Journal
- Shopping with friends
- Meaningful talk with a friend, relative or spouse

Action steps –

1. Practice removing any outside stressors from your life, your schedule or your environment

2. Practicing box breathing and meditations. Try to aim for 1 time per day at least 2 rounds.

3. Pick 1-2 self-care items and put those on your schedule as a sacred meeting with yourself that is a non-negotiable meaning you will not break it for any reason.

What are you Aha's and appreciations for this week? **Be kind to yourself**. A lot of change is happening and acknowledging yourself for these accomplishments big or small will serve as the fuel that will guide you to keep going when times get tough. You got this girl. Keep up the great work!

Client Action Guide - Week 7

What went well this week-

_____
_____
_____
_____

Were you able to honor the 20 minute meal-

_____
_____
_____
_____

Were you able to time your meals appropriately-

_____
_____
_____
_____

If so, how did that make you feel-

_____
_____
_____
_____

What are the major stressors in your life-

_____
_____
_____
_____

What can you change and delegate to make things easier and less stressful?

_____

_____

_____

_____

Where in your life can you eliminate challenges and shift perspective, so stress doesn't negatively affect you and your ability to conceive?

_____

_____

_____

_____

How many times are you going to meditate this week and practice box breathing-

_____

_____

_____

_____

The self-care I plan to do this week is –

_____

_____

_____

_____

All About Stress

BONUS SECTION

In our hectic, busy lives, it seems like stress is just another part of living. While we know that stress is bad for us, so many of us feel like there is nothing we can do about it. Who has time for self-care these days?

When we do not take intentional care of our body, mind, and spirit, it can become very challenging to handle what life throws at us. Our cup empties. Our fuse gets short. We have little energy and motivation. Issues feel bigger than they really are. We are overwhelmed, and the everyday stress we deal with seems almost impossible to get a handle on.

I get it. I've been there.

As a busy mompreneur of two boys with a full-time health coaching practice as well as a full-time workout schedule, I am the first one to be overcome by stress.

In this section, I share with you some simple strategies, tips, and tools to reduce and manage stress in your daily life. I encourage you to choose one or two items from each section and give them a try. Then try others. See what works for you and your routine and do what feels good. YOU are worth this time and devotion! When we take intentional and loving care of ourselves, we are better able to serve and support others.

So, dive in and be sure to reach out to me if you need additional support. I am here to help you live a life that is filled with vitality and joy, and learning to care for yourself and manage stress is an essential step.

Manage Your Stress

Wake up and realize you've overslept...again...

You forgot to pick up dry cleaning, so you don't have anything ready to wear...

Scrambling to get lunch packed, and out the door for work (Where are my keys??) ...

Sitting in traffic...late to work again...

It's not even 9:00 AM! You still have the whole day ahead of you, and you're already stressed out!

Sound familiar?

Stress affects every part of your health, physical and mental. Excess stress can lead to:

- o Poor sleep and insomnia
- o Lowered immune health and frequent illnesses
- o Poor digestive health
- o Anxiety and depression
- o Higher risk of cardiovascular disease, high blood pressure, and obesity
- o Damaged relationships, poor work performance, and a decrease in mental clarity

Stress can lead to chronic inflammation and illness, so it's vital to your health to learn how to manage stress in your life.

What Causes Stress?

The causes of stress are different for everyone. What initiates a stress response for you may not in someone else, while something you take in stride may completely overwhelm another. Also, your physical and mental response to stress is completely individualized. While stress can lead to insomnia for some, others find stress exhausting, and so forth.

Stress can come from many sources - illness, finances, relationships, simply having too much to do, and even excess toxicity can cause or make stress worse. Our society is so pressured and fast-paced that more of us are suffering from stress than ever before, and this stress is leading to more chronic health issues, including chronic inflammation, high blood pressure, obesity, anxiety, and autoimmune disease.

How Can We Manage and Reduce Stress?

Reducing your stress level is often easier said than done. Often, the causes of stress, such as a high-pressure job or a busy schedule can't be avoided.

However, a lack of self-love and self-care often leads to everyday pressures causing more severe stress reactions. By not taking the time to reconnect with your needs or care for yourself both physically and mentally, you're not able to operate as effectively. When you take the time to be mindful of your needs and to lovingly take care of yourself, you are much better able to manage the stressors in your life.

Here are some of my favorite stress management and self-care tools:

- Eat a well-balanced diet. How you nourish your body directly impacts how you can manage stress. By eating nutrient-dense foods that balance your blood sugar, fill you with energy, and boost your immune health, you will have higher levels of physical and mental energy to tackle tasks. Caffeine, sugar, and processed foods make you feel fatigued, lower your immune health, harm your adrenal function which directly affects your stress response, and causes inflammation in the body, so it's important to limit or avoid these foods.

- Deep breathing exercises. Practicing deep breathing exercises is an effective way to calm your central nervous system and can bring focus and clarity to your mind. Practice my 5-5-7 Breathing Technique because not only is it simple, it works! This is a beginner's meditation breathing exercise and you can see demonstrations of this on YouTube.

- Progressive muscular relaxation eases both physical and mental tension. While it's best to do lying down, you can really do this anywhere. Beginning at your head, contract each muscle group for two to four seconds and then release. Move to the next muscle group. Do this all the way down your body until you have contracted, held, and released each muscle group. Finish with a couple of long deep breaths. This is a great way to relax your mind and body to promote restful sleep!

- Keep a gratitude journal. This is something you can do at the beginning or end of each day to help foster positivity and ease negative emotions. Simply take a few moments to write down three things you are grateful for while you are writing. Don't feel like you must write down anything deep; it just has to be authentic. Consistently expressing gratitude for what you have at the moment, has been shown to be a very powerful mindset tool which can lead to decreasing stress over the long term

- Take a break from media. Watching the news, reality shows or intense television dramas can increase stress levels, and so can social media. Because we are so constantly tuned in, media can be overwhelming. Unplug for a week and enjoy reading a book or magazine, spend time outside, or try crafting or creative activities. You may be surprised by how good you feel and how much more productive you are!

- Get connected. Reach out to friends and family for support. This is especially important if you are suffering from chronic health conditions when it's common to feel isolated or alone. If you're struggling with finding the support you need to make changes in your health, look for either a local community or an online community for support.

- Look for the lighter side. Laughter is an amazing cure for stress. When you laugh, your body reduces cortisol, easing the feeling of stress, and your immune system gets a boost. Laughter releases endorphins and increases oxygen to organs. Hang out with your friends, see a funny movie, watch YouTube videos of your favorite comedian, or head to the library for a book that will make you laugh out loud.

- Connect with nature. Getting outside will not only give you a boost of Vitamin D but being in nature is very calming to the nervous system. Try "earthing," also called "grounding," which is simply walking barefoot in the grass to connect your bare skin to the earth. According to the Earthing Institute, "Connection with the Earth restores a lost electrical signal to the body that seems to stabilize the complicated circuitry of our essentially-electrical body. Our built-in, self-regulating and self-healing mechanisms become more effective. There are head-to-toe improvements. Better blood flow. Less pain and inflammation. More energy. Deeper sleep."

- Get in touch with your creativity. Set aside time each week where you can be completely immersed in an activity without worrying about time or interruption and let your creative side free! Whether it's dancing, drawing, coloring, crafting, cooking, woodwork, music - find the creative flow that brings you joy and helps you relax.

- Help others. Random acts of kindness, from volunteering with a charity or organization to picking up the person's coffee behind you at the Starbucks drive-thru, release good feelings and bring joy to others!

- Be kind to yourself. Talk to yourself like you talk to your best friend, with kindness and love. So, you burned dinner, or you were late to pick your child up from dance class - these things happen. Give yourself grace and know you don't have to be perfect.

NOTES

NOTES

NOTES

NOTES

I started working with Christy and Tony about a year ago when they first came to me after a few years of trying to conceive. They were frustrated and beyond exhausted. They had tried EVERYTHING, and nothing was working. After learning a little more about both of them, we got to work making simple changes in both of their diets and lifestyle habits.

Christy was having some problems with PCOS and thought natural fertility might not work for her.

After changing her diet and recommending two natural supplements, [Active Bee Power] which I suggested she add to her fertility smoothies. As well as, royal jelly and she is happy to announce that she is now 12 weeks pregnant with her second. Although she did wind up needing an IUI, the steps she took to prepare her body naturally before that were a big help

Christy and Tony couldn't be happier with the results and urge anyone on the fence to give coach Kela a try. You will be so happy you did.

"I only wish I had found her sooner", Christy R.

"I didn't come this far to only come this far!"

- Mike Kremling

Chapter 9

Sleep Puzzle Piece

*This chapter is compatible with **Week 8** of The Hormone Puzzle Online Coaching program.*

(www.hormonepuzzle.com)

Hey beautiful! It's time to start week 8 and I am so proud of you. You are almost finished with this program and you are probably pregnant by now. If you are not, please don't worry. I promise as you complete this book and continue doing all the action steps,

YOU WILL GET PREGNANT!

I have faith in you and in this process. Let's start this session with what is going well. What went well last week? Did you practice removing any stressors from your environment, did you practice your meditation and box breathing? What self-care did you do? Write all these things down in your journal. Great job!

Hopefully, by this point, you are pregnant. If not, know that it is coming, and you have put yourself in the optimal state to conceive a healthy baby. Know that trying to conceive is a process that can take many years but the tips I have shared in my online course and through this book will prepare your body to conceive naturally or will help any fertility treatment you are undergoing work better.

You are in charge of your destiny.

You have the power to do everything you can to conceive and I hope I have helped you on this journey. If you feel you need a little more and want to continue working with me, I do one-one coaching. If you are interested in this, please go to my website and fill out an application. If you are selected, one of my team members or I, will call you for an interview and talk further about the next steps.

This final week we are going to talk about the last piece of this hormone puzzle.

Sleep

Sleep is just as important as what you eat or how much stress you are under.

During sleep, your body is in an optimal state for healing and creating life. Sleep is a powerful ally in helping to promote optimal fertility as it helps lower adrenal overactivity, balance fertility hormones, boost the immune system, increases stress-resilience and enhances overall health.

Tips for high-quality sleep -

- o Practice the regular rhythms of sleep -- go to bed and wake up at the same time each day

- o No TV in the bedroom

- o Create an aesthetic environment in your bedroom that encourages sleep by using serene and restful colors and eliminating clutter and distraction (Tip: avoid family photos in your bedroom decor for even more of a spa-like feel)

- o Create total darkness and quiet - consider using eye shades and earplugs

- o Avoid caffeine or reduce it after noon -- it may make sleep worse

- o Avoid alcohol -- it helps you get to sleep but makes your sleep interrupted and of poor quality

- o Get regular exposure to daylight for at least 20 minutes daily. The light from the sun enters your eyes and triggers your brain to release specific chemicals and hormones like melatonin that are vital to healthy sleep, mood, and aging

- o Eat no later than two hours before bed -- eating a heavy meal prior to bed will lead to a bad night's sleep and will impede the body's overnight detoxification process

- Write your worries down. During your Power Down Hour, write down the things that are causing you anxiety and make plans for what you might have to do the next day to reduce your worry. It will free up your mind and energy to move into a deep and restful sleep

- Take a hot salt or aromatherapy bath. Raising your body temperature before bed helps to induce sleep. A hot bath also relaxes your muscles and reduces tension physically and psychically. By adding ½ to 1 cup of Epsom salt (magnesium sulfate) and ½ to 1 cup of baking soda (sodium bicarbonate) to your bath, you will gain the benefits of magnesium absorbed through your skin and the alkaline-balancing effects of the baking soda, both of which help with sleep

- Get a massage, stretch or have sex before bed

- Warm your middle with a hot water bottle, which raises your core temperature and helps trigger the proper chemistry for sleep

- Avoid medications that interfere with sleep. These include sedatives (these are used to treat insomnia, but ultimately lead to dependence and disruption of normal sleep rhythms and architecture), antihistamines, stimulants, cold medication, steroids, headache medication that contains caffeine

- Take relaxing minerals such as magnesium and calcium

- Get a relaxing tape or CD to help you get to sleep

- If you experience excessive daytime sleepiness, fatigue, snoring, and have been seen to stop breathing in the middle of the night by your spouse or partner, then consider getting tested for a sleep disorder, such as sleep apnea

ACTION STEPS -

Practice making sleep a priority and aiming for 6-8 hours a night. Practice my sleep tips and decide if you want to move into a 1-1 program with me so you can reach your goals of being a mom quicker and with ease.

Empowering Lessons

What are the most empowering lessons or realizations you want to take with you from this program? Write down 5 of the most important moments and lessons you took from these last 60 days.

1.
_____

I learned:
_____

2.
_____

I learned:
_____

3.
_____

I learned:
_____

4.
_____

I learned:
_____

5.
_____

I learned:
_____

Client Action Guide - Week 8

What stressors did you remove from your environment-

_____
_____
_____

Did you practice meditation, If so, how did it go-

_____
_____
_____

What self-care did you do-

_____
_____
_____

What sleep tips are you going to try this week-

_____
_____
_____

How many hours are you currently sleeping-

_____
_____
_____

How many hours are you aiming for this week-

_____

What will stop you from reaching this goal-

_____
_____
_____

NOTES

NOTES

NOTES

NOTES

Client Testimonial   - Becky and Scott S.

When this couple came to me, they were at the end of their ropes. They had been trying unsuccessfully for many years and thought that they would never become parents. Becky had recently had a miscarriage and Scott was over 40. My program was their last shot.

Becky decided to have it naturally at home without the aid of medications. Her doctor treated it as something normal and said she should wait at least 3 months and try again. Since she and her husband didn't want to just wait and do nothing, they decided to give my program a try. We started with my fertility cleanse which helped cleanse her body after having an IUD for so long (which is what she attributes to her miscarriage). She knew the importance of cleansing her body so she can allow it to do what it is supposed to do naturally.

Although she was extremely nervous that this wouldn't work, she trusted the process, her body and me and knew that it was worth a shot.

After a few months of my protocol, I am happy to announce that she became pregnant!

She and Scott were over the moon.

Her baby was born one day before Thanksgiving and almost 1 year to the day of her miscarriage. She was so thankful and couldn't be happier with my program.

"My advice to you is to follow Coach Kela's advice, be kind to yourself, listen to your body and never give up, it will happen for you, just like it did for us"

- Becky

Chapter 10

BONUS CHAPTER - Supplements Puzzle Piece

** This chapter is compatible with **Bonus Week** of The Hormone Puzzle Online Coaching program. **

(www.hormonepuzzle.com)

Throughout this book and my online classes, I have talked about the importance of whole food nutrition and introduced you to specific lifestyle changes that will put your body into the optimal state for conception and increase your chances of becoming pregnant naturally. What happens if it is still not working? What happens if you are doing all these things, your doctor says there is no medical reason why you aren't getting pregnant and you still aren't seeing the results you want?

Usually, that means that there is an underlying cause or deficiency that we haven't addressed yet.

I will always encourage you to get your vitamins and minerals from a whole foods diet, however, there will usually still be holes. Vitamins and minerals that keep the body functioning properly, including those that are in high demand during pregnancy. These aid in the rapid cell division and development of vital organs such as the baby's brain and your placenta during the first stage of pregnancy.

I would consider throwing out any prenatal vitamin that isn't professional or pharmaceutical grade and investing in one of much higher quality and that will be beneficial and usable by your body.

Target, Rite Aid, Walgreens, Wal-Mart, Costco, etc. does not sell prenatal vitamins that I would consider high enough quality to take myself or to recommend to my clients. You will find high-quality vitamins locally at Whole Foods or any natural food store or on Amazon. My favorite website to order pharmaceutical grade vitamins is from https://us.fullscript.com/welcome/coachkela (practitioner dispensary where you can find my favorite professional-grade products for fertility).

Although I customize my recommendations for each client based on what they need and the issues they are facing, there are a few core supplements that I recommend to pretty much everyone. I have listed these below by category. Infertility, hormone imbalance and optimal health. Please consult your doctor before you begin any supplements to make sure they are aligned with his/her treatment plan as well as do your own research.

Be gentle to yourself, you are doing the best you can.

Below are my suggestions for core supplements when treating these conditions-

Infertility

These are listed by order of importance. If you can't take them all, then pick the top one and start there; then add as needed.

1. Fertile Garden –

   These Chinese herbs replenish the yin of the liver and kidneys, regulates the Flow of Liver Qi, addresses problems that many women face when attempting to conceive in their middle thirties and early forties and regulates the menstrual cycle.

2. Lean and Pure- Pre and Probiotic –

   Probiotics can provide your body with a much-needed balance of "good" bacteria within the digestive tract and help keep you, and your gut healthy while improving food absorption and overall digestion. Prebiotic & Probiotic offers the live bacteria of a Probiotic combined with the bacterial energy sourcing of a Prebiotic to help deliver optimal digestive health.

3. Carlson Labs Fish Oil Multi –

   The omega 3's and 6's found in fish oil help to improve **ovulation**. Consumption of DHA **fatty acids** has shown an increase in progesterone, which is a hormone that regulates the condition of the lining of the uterus and is essential **to** pregnancy. DHA consumption has also shown a decrease in anovulation. These essential fatty acids will also increase the egg quality and the health of the ovarian reserve of mothers of advanced age.

4. Integrated Therapeutics CoQ10 –

Although this is a newer supplement and hasn't been studied for as long as the others have, my clients see great results adding this one in. CoQ10 is necessary for the production of cellular energy. Supplementation is especially important in supporting the high energy needs of the cardiovascular and neurological systems. CoQ10 also supports immune function and skin and periodontal health.

During pre-conception and when dealing with infertility...

*...CoQ10 is important because it plays an essential role in **helping** the mitochondria produce energy used by the cells. ... **CoQ10** is also an antioxidant. In research on **CoQ10** fertility, **egg quality** appears to **improve** by **CoQ10's** action in **egg** cells during IVF.*

5. Pure Encapsulations- Inositol Powder –

Inositol is formulated to support healthy central nervous system function. As a result, Inositol may lessen mild and occasional nervous tension and support healthy mood, emotional wellness and behavior. It also supports healthy ovulatory activity, ovarian function, and reproductive system function.

6. Megafood Daily Maca plus for women –

Maca is used to promote overall health and vitality in women. It is a nourishing superfood found in the mountains of Peru, with chaste tree berry, a time-honored botanical shown to help maintain hormonal health and ease symptoms associated with menstruation. It is also shown that Maca helps suppress estrogen dominance and encourage a favorable estrogen/progesterone balance conducive to achieving pregnancy. Many women also report an increase in libido and sexual function when taking Maca which is also a HUGE plus when trying to get pregnant. Maca has also shown to increase semen quality in both fertile and infertile men. This amazing superfood does SO much and tastes great. Add it to your smoothies, shakes, in baked goods, etc.

7. Now Foods, Royal Jelly –

Imagine finding the ultimate fertility enhancer; one that could strengthen the health of your eggs and make conception more likely. If you are finding it difficult to get pregnant, take a cue from the everyday bee. The queen bee is responsible for laying up to 2,000 eggs per day to keep the hive viable. This requires extreme health and fertility. That is why the nurse bees feed her **Royal Jelly,**

…an extremely nutritious gel excreted from the glands of young worker bees and found within the hive.

It is this jelly that helps the queen live six times longer than the average worker bee and be able to produce eggs at a tremendous rate.

While Royal Jelly will not increase your egg production, it may help to strengthen your eggs, making them more likely to fertilize and implant within the uterus. Containing a complex blend of amino acids, vitamins, essential enzymes, sterols, proteins and sugars, not to mention essential fatty acids, iron and calcium, royal jelly supplements may help to:

- regulate your period
- make ovulation more predictable
- strengthen your eggs
- increase sperm counts in men
- protect female eggs and male sperm from free radicals
- increase sperm health and motility
- reduces inflammation throughout the body

Plus the benefits listed above, new research indicates that Royal jelly also contains an estrogen type property that can help to regulate hormone levels in women with too little estrogen. It has been used successfully in women with **Polycystic Ovarian Syndrome** and scanty periods to rebalance their hormones and help them conceive.

Of course, anyone who is allergic to bees or bee stings should not use any type of Royal jelly supplement.

Hormone Imbalance

These are listed by order of importance. If you can't take them all then pick the top one and start there, then add as needed. These are the supplements I recommend to my clients struggling to balance their hormones in a more natural way.

1. Dr. Mercola Premium Products - Whole Food Multivitamin PLUS –

   Proper nutrient balance -- just like too little of a nutrient does not provide you any real benefits, too much can potentially do you more harm than good.

   Absorbability -- the key to promoting your health is absorbing as much of the nutrient as possible. This is why it is SO important to choose a whole food multivitamin because most vitamins you find on the shelves at your local store aren't being absorbed by your body and therefore are a waste of money.

   Allergenic potential -- careful selection and measurement of the nutrient to investigate potential allergy issues.

2. Megafood Daily Maca plus for women –

   Maca is used to promote overall health and vitality in women. It is a nourishing superfood found in the mountains of Peru, with chaste tree berry, a time-honored botanical shown to help maintain hormonal health and ease symptoms associated with menstruation.

   Maca helps balance levels of the hormone estrogen.

   One study found that postmenopausal women who took maca daily experienced reduced symptoms, such as hot flashes and night sweats. Maca also stimulates the endocrine system helping to maintain hormonal balance.

3. Lean and Pure- Pre and Probiotic –

Emerging research indicates that the gut microbiome plays a central role in the regulation of estrogen levels within the body and thus influences the risk of developing estrogen-related diseases such as endometriosis, polycystic ovary syndrome, breast cancer, and prostate cancer. Adding a pre and probiotic supplement to your daily routine will help balance your gut microbiome and regulate your hormones.

When balancing hormones there are many factors involved depending on where you are off. When working with me in my 1-1 coaching program we look at where you are off and I recommend supplements accordingly to help you balance your hormones.

Since these are recommended on a case by case individual basis please reach out to me with further questions at info@kelahealthcoach.com.

In postmenopausal women, estrobolome disruption is associated with an increased risk of obesity, cardiovascular disease, and osteoporosis.

Estrogens regulate glucose and lipid metabolism, adipocyte differentiation, bone formation, and the inflammatory response in atherosclerosis. Research indicates that the normal reductions in estrogen that occurs at menopause impair these estrogen-dependent processes, triggering obesity, cardiovascular disease, and osteoporosis.

Endometriosis, an estrogen-driven condition characterized by the growth of endometrial tissue outside the uterus, has been associated with gut dysbiosis.

The estrobolome of women with endometriosis may have larger numbers of beta-glucuronidase-producing bacteria, leading to increased levels of circulating estrogen, which drives endometriosis.

Polycystic ovary syndrome (PCOS) may also be influenced by estrobolome disruption. Women with PCOS have an excess of androgens in relation to estrogen, as well as altered gut microbiota.

Researchers theorize that the altered gut microbiota in PCOS women may promote increased androgen biosynthesis and decreased estrogen levels through lowered beta-glucuronidase activity.

I recommend a prebiotic and probiotic supplement to all my clients whether you are struggling with infertility, hormone imbalance or you just want to have overall optimal great health.

Optimal Health

These are the supplements I recommend for anyone wanting optimal great health. These are the basics. Of course, you can supplement in many different areas with many different products, however, these or ones similar should be your baseline. Like if you can only afford certain supplements these 3 should be on the top of the list. These are listed by order of importance. Choose to take them all or only the top ones.

Dr. Mercola Premium Products – Whole Food Multivitamin PLUS –

Proper nutrient balance -- just like too little of a nutrient does not provide you any real benefits, too much can potentially do you more harm than good. The reason to choose a whole food multivitamin is that you want the vitamins and minerals to be bio-available for your body and as close to nature as possible.

Many of the vitamin supplements you find on the supermarket shelves are man-made in a laboratory and your body doesn't know what to do with them, so it flushes them out through your bowels without ever getting the benefit of the vitamin in the first place. Not to mention it's flushing your hard-earned money down the drain. When choosing a multivitamin, make sure you choose a whole food one.

Absorbability -- the key to promoting your health is absorbing as much of the nutrient as possible. This is why it is SO important to choose a whole food multivitamin because most vitamins you find on the shelves at your local store aren't being absorbed by your body and therefore are a waste of money.

Allergenic potential -- careful selection and measurement of the nutrient to investigate potential allergy issues.

Lean and Pure – Pre and Probiotic –

Probiotics are the good bacteria living in your gut. (You have both good and bad bacteria in your body, and a balance is necessary for a healthy gut.)

Probiotics help you in a variety of ways:

- They break down and digest food.
- They support overall gut health.
- They ensure the immune system works well.
- They also play a role in how you think and feel. Gut bacteria can improve the production and regulation of hormones, such as insulin and leptin. And they have been found to produce neurotransmitters, such as serotonin, dopamine, and GABA — which play a key role in your mood.

Prebiotics are the food for the good bacteria. They come from the non-digestible fiber in certain plant-based foods.

With names such as oligosaccharides, galactooligosaccharide, and inulin.

They stimulate the growth and activity of your body's beneficial bacteria (probiotics). All prebiotics are fiber, but not all fiber is prebiotic.

You need both probiotics and prebiotics. They work together to support your microbiome…

…the community of trillions of bacteria in your body that helps it function properly.

It's a synergistic relationship. Without prebiotics as fuel, probiotics would starve — leaving you open to a host of problems, such as leaky gut, a compromised immune system, and constipation. And with no probiotics around to eat them, prebiotics would be of little value to your gut.

Adding a pre and probiotic to your diet will greatly improve your health and wellbeing.

My recommendations are you start with food first and then fill in holes where you need it depending on what you are struggling with. Work with a coach or your doctor in finding the right supplement combination for you. Once you start to nail down your intentional diet and begin to implement all the action steps and protocols in this book, your body will become optimized for fertility and you will become pregnant naturally.

"She thought she could, so she did"

- R.S. Grey

Chapter 11

BONUS CHAPTER - **PCOS Puzzle Piece**

I have decided to include a few chapters on the most common causes of infertility in this book as a bonus. This information isn't in my online course yet (although I might add it in the future). As I was writing this book clients kept coming to me struggling with these issues so I wanted to address them and show you what the symptoms are and how to start reversing them so you can put your body into that optimal state for conception no matter what your diagnosis.

Polycystic Ovary Syndrome (PCOS)

Polycystic ovary syndrome, also known as polycystic ovary disease (PCOD) affects five to ten percent of women in North America and is the leading cause of ovulatory based infertility.

Women with PCOS have high levels of male hormones (androgens) which interfere with the normal production of female hormones like estrogen. This results in the ovaries filling with cysts or creating immature follicles that are unable to generate eggs.

Along with reduced fertility women with PCOS are at a heightened risk for:

- o ü Type 2 Diabetes
- o ü Heart Disease
- o ü Some forms of cancer

What are the symptoms?

Some women with PCOS have no symptoms. More often, however, women will experience some or all the following symptoms:

- ü Weight gain or obesity

- ü Excessive hair growth (hirsutism) and/or abnormal hair growth

- ü Irregular periods or complete absence of menstruation (amenorrhea)

- ü Acne

- ü Enlarged ovaries covered with cysts

- ü Insulin resistance/hyperinsulinemia

How is PCOS diagnosed?

If your medical doctor suspects that you have PCOS she may recommend that you have a blood test to test for elevated LH (luteinizing hormone) and serum testosterone and an ultrasound of the ovaries to determine if cysts are present (about 20% of all women will have ovarian cysts visible on the ultrasound, so having the cysts does not necessarily mean you have PCOS).

From a Chinese medicine perspective, it is always important to look at the individual pattern diagnosis. Your practitioner will do a thorough evaluation of physical and emotional signs and symptoms as well as analyzing your diet and lifestyle and checking your tongue and pulse in order to determine what your specific needs are.

What is the cause?

No one knows the exact cause of PCOS.

Women with PCOS frequently have a mother or sister with the condition but there is not yet enough evidence to say there is a genetic link to this disorder. Many women with PCOS have a weight problem. So researchers are looking at the relationship between PCOS and the body's ability to use insulin.

PCOS often results in increased insulin resistance, glucose intolerance, impaired glucose metabolism, elevated lipid profile, high blood pressure, mood swings, and irritability.

This means that the body has a reduced capacity to metabolize insulin and glucose.

The pancreas works harder to produce insulin, but the insulin cannot do its work of transporting glucose (sugar) into the cells because of a hormonal imbalance or because of too many fat cells.

The excess insulin in the blood leads to excess glucose in the blood and sets the conditions for prediabetes, weight gain and diabesity. **If untreated, PCOS can lead to obesity, heart disease, diabetes, and some cancers.**

How does insulin affect fertility?

Insulin is a hormone that regulates the change of sugar, starches, and other food into energy for the body's use or for storage. Excess insulin causes a rise in male hormones which can lead to

- acne
- excessive hair growth
- weight gain
- ovulation problems

As well, insulin blocks the liver from producing sex hormone binding globulin --a hormone that restricts which cells are affected by testosterone. High insulin levels increase the amount of male hormones circulating in the blood and amplifies the effects of these hormones on all the cells.

In turn, high levels of insulin stimulate the ovaries to overproduce androgens. Excess androgens cause the follicles to develop too quickly & then to shut down prematurely before they produce an egg.

To make matters worse insulin sensitivity contributes to gain weight, especially in the belly area, and makes it harder to lose weight.

If that wasn't bad enough this excess fat sets up a negative feedback system: The adipocyte or fat derived hormone leptin inhibits the stimulatory effect of FHS.

Obesity is associated with gonotrophic resistance. This is a classic example of too much yang and not enough yin. In Chinese medicine, this condition can have a number of linked patterns of deficiency and excess that have an impact on the way the body ovulates.

How is PCOS treated?

Treatment depends on the severity of the condition. For both Western and Chinese medicine, the first line of treatment is diet and weight control. With some women, reducing insulin levels and improving insulin sensitivity through weight loss, a low glycemic diet and exercise may restore normal ovulation.

For more severe cases, Western treatment may also include fertility drugs, insulin regulating drugs and, in some cases, assisted reproductive therapies like In vitro fertilization. I always start with diet and lifestyle changes first, and then if we don't get the results, we want we will add more western medicine protocols.

The Chinese approach is to treat the underlying condition that is causing the hormonal imbalance as well as to alleviate symptoms. Typically, a personalized treatment plan to rebalance hormones and regulate the menstrual period takes approximately 3 to 6 months.

As mentioned, diet and lifestyle play a crucial role in treating PCOS. The goal is to regulate blood sugar, decrease insulin resistance and improve glucose metabolism.

This will help to stabilize insulin levels, moods and weight. Following an anti-inflammatory, low glycemic diet can keep your blood sugar stable, improve insulin sensitivity, and reduce phlegm.

Ten tips to kickstart your PCOS –

This is similar to what I teach someone struggling with any sort of infertility, however, these recommendations are specifically for someone struggling with PCOS.

- Eat low Glycemic Index (GI) carbohydrates such as vegetables and whole grains. It is very important for women with PCOS to completely avoid refined carbohydrates including sugar, white flour, whole wheat flour and products made from them *(example: pasta, bread, desserts, soda, and candy)*
- Keep your blood sugar stable with a daily schedule of meals and snacks every three to five hours that includes some protein and good fats (for example some nuts/nut butter, seeds/seed butter, hard-boiled egg, hummus dip). Protein foods take up to 5 hours to digest while carbohydrate foods digest within 30 minutes.
- Eat at least five servings a day of vegetables including two of leafy greens
- Have a daily serving of legumes like black beans or lentils.
- Enjoy grass or pasture-fed meat up to three times a week
- Eat at least three daily servings of fruits like berries, which have a lower glycemic impact. Each serving of fruit should be enjoyed as part of a meal or with a protein.
- Limit or eliminate milk and dairy as these can aggravate internal dampness. If you do
- have dairy have only non-homogenized full-fat milk.
- Pay careful attention to portion sizes in order to moderate glucose load and minimize insulin resistance
- Add one or two Tbsp of cinnamon on cereal each morning to help decrease insulin resistance.
- Include prebiotic and probiotic foods which promote the growth of beneficial bacteria in the intestinal tract. Prebiotics are found in whole grains, onions, bananas, garlic, honey, leeks, artichokes and some fortified foods. Probiotic foods are found in fermented foods (sauerkraut, live culture yogurt, kim chi, miso).
- In addition, get your heart rate up with at least 30 minutes of vigorous exercise every day. Studies have shown that exercise can reverse diabetes and improve insulin sensitivity as well as help with weight control.

Just losing five to ten percent of your body weight if you are overweight, can restore your menstrual periods and reduce distressing symptoms like facial hair and acne.

However, it is important not to exercise too hard. Over exercise depletes your yin and can raise your testosterone levels. This is not the time to start your marathon training. Balance is the key especially if you are struggling with PCOS.

Supplements for PCOS

- Chlorophyll: reduces symptoms of hypoglycemia without raising blood glucose level
- B vitamins, magnesium, alpha lipoic acid and conjugated linoleic acid: improve insulin resistance
- N-acetylcysteine (NAC) - Regulates blood sugar and is a strong antioxidant
- Saw Palmetto - blocks the production of DHT (dihydrotestosterone)
- Bitter Melon and fenugreek - Regulate blood glucose

In general, lifestyle changes which include weight loss, insulin control and TCM treatment with herbs and acupuncture have proven to be very effective in the treatment of PCOS.

After a couple of months of treatment, you should notice signs of ovulation like increased mid- month vaginal discharge and elevated Basal Body Temperature (BBT).

You may notice, if you have very long cycles, that ovulation comes earlier in the cycle indicating healthier egg production. You will also see that your quality of skin improves, and excess hair will diminish.

Chapter 12

BONUS CHAPTER – Endometriosis Puzzle Piece

Endometriosis affects 10 – 15 percent of women between the ages of 24 and 40 years of age.

The triad of symptoms includes dysmenorrhea (pain during menses); dyspareunia (pain with intercourse) and infertility.

Endometriosis is the growth of endometrial tissue in other areas of a woman's body besides the uterus. This tissue is usually found in the abdomen – on the ovaries, fallopian tubes, the ligaments that support the uterus, between the vagina and rectum, the outside of the uterus or the lining of the pelvic cavity – but also sometimes on the bladder, bowel, vagina, cervix and vulva; and very rarely, in the lungs, arms and legs.

The cause of endometriosis is not clear, but it has been strongly linked to immune system dysfunction and exposure to dioxins and other toxic chemicals that accumulate in the fat stores of fish, animals and people.

The puzzle method is recommended as an adjunct treatment for endometriosis in addition to hormonal treatment. The priority is to first minimize PCB and dioxin exposure and consumption in the home, workplace and diet. A thorough detoxification program along with an anti-inflammatory diet is recommended with an emphasis on the following:

- Use high fiber foods which increase transit time in the intestines and promote an optimal balance of probiotics in the intestines.
- Avoid meat because it contains large amounts of arachidonic acid with promotes inflammatory prostaglandins and inflammation and pain.
- Increase liver friendly foods such as kale, Brussels sprouts, broccoli, rapini.
- Use more anti-inflammatory spices such as turmeric (which protects against environmental carcinogens and decreases inflammation); ginger, milk thistle seeds, ground flaxseeds.
- Avoid sugar, caffeine and alcohol.
- Avoid/minimize dairy products (they cause the lipid pathway to be tipped toward prostaglandins and leukotrienes that cause inflammation and vascular constriction).
- Supplement the diet with fish oil to help to reduce pain symptoms and decrease the inflammatory response. Choose only supplements from an approved source that has proven low mercury, short lived, deep water fish

The Closing –

Congratulations you have made it to the end of these 8 weeks. I am so proud of you, you did it. You are one step closer to having the baby and the life you have always wanted. It hasn't been easy, nor will it continue to be. However, with constant and consistent action you will put your body into the optimal state for conception and allow it to do what it is designed to do, naturally. During this journey, it is not about being perfect or doing all the steps perfectly. It is about progress, doing one thing every day that will move you forward.

Will you hit roadblocks, *absolutely.*

Will some days you just want to say fuck it and stay in bed and eat Ben and Jerry's fudge brownie (ok maybe that was just me)?

That is ok though, as long as you continue to move forward, and focus on your why,

Dig into that why when times get hard.

It's not just important to know you want a baby. You want to get pregnant and have a healthy baby but knowing why you want that will allow your brain to go deeper, it will solidify the reasons for doing all this and make your resolve that much stronger. Lean on your family and friends. They have you, I have you, you got this, you are stronger than you think.

Now let's go make some babies.

Client Action Guide - Week 8

What stressors did you remove from your environment-

_____

_____

_____

Did you practice meditation, If so, how did it go-

_____

_____

_____

What self-care did you do-

_____

_____

_____

What sleep tips are you going to try this week-

_____

_____

_____

How many hours are you currently sleeping-

_____

_____

_____

How many hours are you aiming for this week-

_____

_____

_____

What will stop you from reaching this goal-

_____

_____

_____

Holiday's were always hard for us because I always wanted to enjoy family dinner and cook a huge meal for everyone, however, I love eating healthy and didn't want to compromise my values or my waistline during the holidays, especially when I was trying to get pregnant because what I was eating was playing such a huge role in being able to conceive.

That is why I wanted to add a bonus section in this book for holiday recipes.

These are the ones I used during that trying time in our lives of trying to conceive. You know what surprised me, ***EVERYONE LOVED THEM.*** I wanted to share some of my favorites here with you in the hopes that your family will love them as much as we do. Happy cooking!

Holiday Recipes

Recipe Guide

Main Course

Herb Roasted Turkey with Garlic Butter and Gravy

Side Dish

Creamy Mashed Potatoes

Melt in your mouth Roasted Sweet Potatoes

Butternut Squash Salad

Easy, Delicious Scalloped Potatoes

Happy Holiday Beet Salad

Gorgeous Green Beans

Dessert

Pumpkin Pie Mousse

Healthy Buckeye Cookies

Coconut Date Balls

Herb Roasted Turkey with Garlic Butter and Gravy

[Main Course]

Ingredients:

- 1 12-14-pound whole turkey, giblets + neck removed, rinsed + patted dry
- 6 fresh sage leaves, divided
- 5 fresh thyme sprigs, divided
- 2 sprigs fresh rosemary
- 3 medium organic onions, cut into wedges
- 5 medium organic carrots, cut into 2-inch pieces
- 4 organic celery ribs, cut into 2-inch pieces
- 1 organic lemon, halved
- 4 cups low-sodium chicken broth or homemade chicken bone broth

Garlic Herb Butter:

- ¾ cup unsalted grass-fed butter, at room temperature
- 1-½ TBSP chopped fresh rosemary
- 1-½ TBSP chopped fresh sage
- 1-½ TBSP chopped fresh thyme leaves
- 1 TBSP chopped fresh parsley
- 5 cloves garlic minced
- 2-3 tsp Himalayan sea salt
- 1 tsp black pepper

Instructions:

Thaw turkey (if using frozen):

Allow 2 to 3 days for it to fully defrost in the refrigerator. Remove giblets & neck, rinse & pat dry.

Make the garlic herb butter:

In a medium bowl, combine butter, rosemary, sage, thyme, parsley, garlic, salt, and black pepper. Stir together until smooth and combined.

Prep the outside of the turkey:

Carefully loosen the skin from the turkey breast with your hands lifting and separating the meat. Do the same for the neck as well as the thighs and legs. Gently rub half of the butter under the skin using your hands and fingers and place 3 sage leaves and 2 thyme sprigs under the skin. Tie the legs together and tuck the wings underneath the turkey, using small skewers to secure, if necessary.

Prepare the inside of the turkey:

Place ⅓ of the onions, celery, carrots, 2 sage leaves, 2 thyme sprigs, 1 rosemary sprigs and lemon halves inside the cavity of the turkey. Place turkey, breast side up in a large roasting pan. Melt the remaining butter in the microwave and brush an even layer over the skin of the turkey. Arrange remaining carrots, celery and herbs in the pan around the turkey. Pour chicken broth in the bottom of the roasting pan (will be using liquid to baste turkey).

Cook the turkey:

Preheat oven to 425°F and position rack in the lower third of the oven. Once the oven is ready, place the roasting pan with the turkey into the oven and cook for 45 minutes uncovered.

After 45 minutes, reduce the oven temperature to 350°F and continue to roast until a meat thermometer (inserted deep into the thigh but away from the bone) reads 180°F and juices in the thigh run clear when pierced with a fork, about 2 to 2.5 hours (or longer depending on your oven and size of your turkey), basting with pan broth & drippings every 30 minutes.

Tent with foil the last 30 minutes of cooking:

Cover loosely with foil during the last 30 minutes of cooking or if turkey browns too quickly. Once the turkey is done, remove the pan from the oven. Carefully transfer turkey from the pan onto a baking sheet and allow to rest for 15 minutes before carving. Strain and reserve pan juices for gravy, if desired, and discard vegetables.

Creamy Mashed Potatoes
[Side Dish]

Ingredients:

- 5-6 large yellow potatoes cut into 1-inch cubes
- 3 TBSP grass fed butter
- 1 whole garlic clove, minced
- Milk or coconut milk to consistency

Instructions:

Boil potatoes until fork tender

Place potatoes in a bowl with all ingredients except milk and blend while slowly adding milk until a creamy consistency is reached.

The skin on or off is your preference

Top with desired toppings- cheese, chives, bacon, mushrooms, etc.

Melt in your mouth Roasted Sweet Potatoes
[Side Dish]

Ingredients:

- 4 sweet potatoes peeled and cubed
- 2 tsp minced garlic
- 1 TBSP olive oil
- 2 TBSP grass fed butter melted
- 4 TBSP grated Parmesan cheese
- 1 TBSP brown sugar
- ½ tsp garlic salt
- ½ tsp Italian Seasoning
- dried parsley

Instructions:

Preheat oven to 400°F.

Peel and cube sweet potatoes into 1-inch cubes.

Place garlic, oil, butter, salt, Parmesan cheese, brown sugar and Italian seasoning in a Ziploc bag and mix well.

Throw in sweet potatoes and shake until well coated.

Place aluminum foil on a cookie sheet and lightly spray.

Place coated sweet potatoes onto a cookie sheet and spread out evenly.

Bake for 18-22 minutes.

Serve warm and sprinkle with dried parsley and more parmesan if desired.

Butternut Squash Salad
[Side Dish]

Roasted Brussels Sprouts:

- 3 cups Brussels sprouts ends trimmed, yellow leaves removed
- 3 TBSP olive oil
- ¼ tsp Salt to taste

Roasted Butternut Squash:

- 1½ lb butternut squash peeled, seeded, and cubed into 1-inch cubes (Yields about 4 cups of uncooked cubed butternut squash)
- 2 TBSP olive oil
- 3 TBSP pure maple syrup
- ½ tsp ground cinnamon
- ½ tsp ground ginger
- 1 TBSP brown sugar

Add all ingredients in a bowl, stir to combine, bake on 375°F for 20 minutes until slightly browned.

Toppings:

- 2 cups pecan halves, pumpkin seeds or walnuts
- 1 cup dried cranberries

Pull from the oven and let cool slightly then put in a serving bowl, top with toppings, stir to combine and enjoy.

Easy, Delicious Scalloped Potatoes

[Side Dish]

Ingredients:

- 2 TBSP grass fed butter melted
- 6 yellow potatoes peeled and sliced into
- ⅛ inch thick slices
- ½ tsp Himalayan salt
- 4 garlic cloves minced
- 1 ¼ cups Parmesan and cheddar cheese shredded
- 3 TBSP Thyme; fresh
- 1 cup of canned coconut milk

Instructions:

Preheat oven to 400°F.

Grease the bottom of the medium casserole pan with melted butter.

Spread ¼ of the sliced potatoes in an even layer on the bottom of the pan. Sprinkle the potatoes with ⅛ tsp salt, then top with 1 minced garlic clove, ¼ cup of grated Parmesan cheese, ¼ amount of thyme leaves (removed from sprigs). Top with ¼ cup of canned coconut milk, pouring it evenly over the potatoes.

Repeat layers 3 more times (total of 4 layers of potatoes). For the last layer, use ½ a cup of shredded Parmesan cheese (or more).

Bake at 400 F, uncovered, for about 1 hour, or until the potatoes are cooked through.

Happy Holiday Beet Salad

[Side Dish]

Ingredients:

- 5 large organic carrots peeled & sliced
- 4 medium organic beets peeled & diced
- 2 TBSP olive oil
- Salt & pepper to taste
- 2 TBSP grass fed butter
- 3 TBSP pure maple syrup
- 2 TBSP of brown sugar

Instructions:

Preheat oven to 425°F and move the rack to the middle position.

Cut the beets and carrots into pieces that are roughly the same size and place the pieces on a large baking sheet.

Drizzle the olive oil onto the beets and carrots and add salt, pepper, & brown sugar. Toss until coated. Spread them out in an even layer.

Roast for about 15 minutes, or until the vegetables are tender-crisp (this will vary depending on how big the pieces are).

Take the baking sheet out of the oven and add the butter and maple syrup directly to the baking sheet. Let the butter melt then toss it again until everything is coated.

Return the baking sheet to the oven for another 5 minutes.

Serve immediately.

Gorgeous Green Beans
[Side Dish]

Ingredients:

- 1 ½ lbs fresh green beans, ends trimmed
- 1 shallot, minced
- 1 TBSP olive oil
- ½ tsp kosher salt
- ⅛ – ¼ tsp garlic powder
- ¼ tsp paprika
- ¼ tsp chili powder
- ¼ tsp freshly ground black pepper
- ¼-⅛ tsp of red pepper (optional)

Instructions:

Preheat oven to 425°F.

Place green beans and shallots on a rimmed sheet pan. Drizzle with olive oil, then sprinkle with salt, garlic powder, paprika, chili powder, pepper and red pepper (if using). Toss beans to coat evenly with oil and seasoning.

Roast green beans for 20 minutes.

Serve warm.

Pumpkin Pie Mousse

[Dessert]

Ingredients:

- 15 oz pumpkin, canned
- 3 can coconut milk, unsweetened
- ½ cup raw honey
- 1 TBSP pure vanilla extract
- 2 ½ TBSP pumpkin pie spice
- ¼ tsp Himalayan salt

Instructions:

REFRIGERATE ALL 3 CANS OF COCONUT MILK OVERNIGHT.

CHILL the bowl of a stand mixer and whisk attachment in the fridge (20+min) or freezer (10 min).

Remove 1 can of coconut milk from the fridge, turn it upside down and open the can. Pour out the clear liquid into a container to store in the refrigerator for later (use in smoothies, soups, etc.). Scoop out the cream with a spoon and place in a medium saucepan.

Add the pumpkin, honey, vanilla, pumpkin pie spice, and salt to the saucepan with the coconut cream. Cook on medium heat until mixture simmers. Reduce heat to low and simmer for 5 minutes, stirring occasionally. Remove from heat and pour into a large bowl that has been placed inside an ice-water bath (another bowl with ice and water). Stir the mixture to cool it faster. Let the bowl of pumpkin sit in the ice-water bath while you work on the next step. It's important to keep everything cold so the pumpkin mousse is stiff instead of soupy.

Once the pumpkin mixture has cooled, prepare the coconut whipped cream. Remove the remaining 2 cans of coconut milk from the refrigerator, turn them upside down and open the cans. Pour out the clear liquid into a container to store in the refrigerator for later. Scoop out the cream with a spoon and place it in the chilled mixing bowl. Attach the whisk to the stand mixer and whip until stiff peaks form, adding 2 stevia packets to sweeten the whipped coconut cream, if desired.

Gently fold in ⅔ to 3/4 of the whipped coconut cream into the pumpkin mixture, being careful not to over-mix.

Fill a pastry bag that has been fitted with a star tip with the pumpkin mixture, and pipe it into 6 to 8 small dessert dishes. Do a little at a time, so you don't warm the mousse too much in the pastry bag with your hands. (You may scoop the mousse into dishes if you don't have a pastry bag.)

Top with a little swirl or dollop of the remaining whipped coconut cream, and a sprinkle of cinnamon, if desired. Chill the pumpkin mousse in the refrigerator for an hour or two before serving. Store in refrigerator up to 1 week in a container with a lid.

Healthy Buckeye Cookies

[Dessert]

Ingredients:

- 1 cup almond flour packed
- ½ cup coconut flour, packed
- ½ cup coconut or brown sugar
- ¾ cup peanut butter (for paleo-friendly or peanut-free sub any nut/seed butter of choice)
- 4 Tbsp coconut oil, melted
- 1 ½ tsp pure maple syrup
- 1½ tsp pure vanilla extract
- pinch of salt

For the melted chocolate:

- ½ – ⅔ cup dark chocolate chips or raw cacao powder
- 1 Tbsp Coconut oil
- Coarse Himalayan sea salt for topping

Instructions:

In a bowl, combine all the dough ingredients. If peanut butter or nut butter is on the thicker side, heat slightly over medium-low heat along with coconut oil until it achieves a smooth flowing consistency.

Once the dough is mixed well, place in the fridge for 15 minutes.

Roll dough into 24 balls, about 1 heaping Tbsp. of dough per ball.

Place on a sheet pan or plate lined with parchment paper

Place dough balls back into the fridge for another 15 minutes.

Over medium-low heat, add the chocolate and coconut oil. Stir continuously until chocolate is melted and smooth.

Remove dough balls from the fridge and dip all but the top of the ball into the chocolate. A toothpick works great for dipping.

If desired, drizzle with leftover melted chocolate and top with a little coarse sea salt.

Serve chilled if possible.

Coconut Date Balls

[Dessert]

Ingredients:

- 2 cups walnuts (or other favorite nuts)
- 2 cups Medjool dates, pitted (about 20-24 dates)
- ½ cup unsweetened shredded coconut
- 2-3 TBSP coconut oil
- 1 tsp Pink Himalayan salt or sea salt
- 1 tsp pure vanilla extract

Instructions:

In a food processor, add all ingredients and process until well blended. *Note you may have to stir up a bit to get all ingredients equally processed.

Using a small ice cream scoop, roll balls in your hand and arrange on a wax paper/parchment paper lined cookie sheet, or place directly in a storage container.

* Optional: Roll in shredded coconut if you are taking these to a party or event. *

Store in the refrigerator or freezer until gone! The freezer will give these a much firmer consistency when you bite into the ball, which I prefer.

The Complete **Hormone Puzzle** COOKBOOK

Your guide to balancing your hormones
and fighting infertility
naturally

Coach Kela Smith

This section is *The Complete Hormone Puzzle Cookbook.*

These recipes are designed to put your body into the optimal state for conception so that you get pregnant naturally.

When I was struggling with infertility, I knew the way I was eating played a huge roll in how my body was able to perform.

That is when I began researching whole food, targeted nutrition and this cookbook was born.

My hope is for you to take your health into your own hands and use these recipes as your guide to put your body into the best possible position to balance your hormones, so you can conceive a healthy baby.

It is possible and you can do it!

Recipe Guide

Breakfast

Fertility Boosting Smoothie
Sunrise Smoothie
Repairing Smoothie Bowl
Raspberry Sunrise Bowl
Satisfying Chia Seed Bowl
Super Food Breakfast Cookie
Yummy Breakfast Casserole
Cherry Detox Smoothie
Strawberry Dream Smoothie
Overnight Oats
Sweet Potato Avocado Toast
Almond Flour Pancakes
Yummy in my Tummy Granola

Soups

Creamy Tomato Soup
Adzuki Bean Soup
Hormone Balancing Bean Soup
Soothing Black Bean Soup
Thai Squash Stew
White Bean Chicken Chili
Bone Broth
Bone Broth Brussel Sprouts

Lunch

Roasted Veggies and Protein
Corn and Black Bean Jar Salad
Super Foods Green Salad
Healthy Taco Bowl
BBQ Chicken Wrap with Ranch
Homemade Ranch
Homemade BBQ Sauce
Tomato Quinoa with Veggies
Fish Tacos
Yummy Jar Salad

Dinner

Spicy Vegan Chili
Quinoa Crust Easy Pizza
Thai Veggie Quinoa Bowls
Sweet Potato/Black Bean Enchiladas
Polenta with Roasted Veggies
Veggie Quesadillas
Coconut Lime Chicken
Roasted Squash and Feta Couscous
Crockpot Melt in Your Mouth Chicken
Sweet Chili Lime Salmon
Grilled Yummy Baked Chicken
Coconut Chicken Tenders
Roasted Veggies and Sausage

Vinaigrettes, Rubs, Seasonings

Apple Cider Vinaigrette
Chicken or Beef Spice Rub
Red Wine Vinaigrette
Easy Detox Pesto
Clean Taco Seasoning
Homemade Almond Milk
Homemade Guacamole

Dessert

Yummy Fertility Brownies
Fudgy Fudge
Edible Cookie Dough
Chocolate Fiber Balls
Almond Butter Brownies
Peanut Butter Mug Cake
Chocolate "Nice" Cream
Berry "Nice" Cream
Almond Butter Energy Balls
Healthy Peanut Butter Cup

Breakfast

Fertility Boosting Smoothie

Ingredients:

- 1 cup frozen cherries
- ½ cup frozen raspberries
- ½ cup frozen spinach
- ½ cup frozen blueberries
- 1 TBSP no sugar added almond butter
- 1 scoop unsweetened pea or rice protein powder (NutriBiotic rice protein is my favorite)
- 1 cup unsweetened almond milk
- A few ice cubes

Directions:

Blend all ingredients in a ninja/blender until smooth.

Serve in a pretty glass with a straw.

(Yields 1 serving)

Progesterone promoting Vitamin C is crucial to help increase progesterone production and is also an important antioxidant necessary in bodily processes, such as protein metabolism and the synthesis of neurotransmitters.

Sunrise Smoothie

Ingredients:

- ½ cup frozen oranges
- ½ cup frozen Papaya
- ½ cup frozen grapefruit
- ½ of a frozen banana
- 1 TBSP almond butter
- 1-2 scoops of pea or rice protein powder
- 1 cup almond or coconut milk
- 1 TBSP flax seeds
- 1 TBSP chia seeds
- Walnuts or pumpkin seeds
- a few ice cubes

Androgen reducing foods such as grapefruit and papaya lower high levels of male hormones like DHEA and testosterone which can reduce the ability to conceive. Signs of excess are susceptibility to acne, experiencing hair loss on the scalp and increased hair growth in atypical areas for females.

Directions:

Blend all ingredients in a ninja/blender and top with a sprinkle of pumpkin seeds or walnuts.

Yield 1 serving

Repairing Green Smoothie Bowl

Ingredients:

- 2 frozen bananas
- ½ frozen avocado
- 1 frozen kiwi
- 2 slices of ginger root
- 2 cups frozen spinach
- 1 tsp cinnamon
- 1 TBSP cashew butter
- ¾ cup coconut drinking milk
- 1-2 TBSP honey or maple syrup
- 2 tsp Spirulina
- Kiwi slices, skin removed
- 1 TBSP flax or chia
- sliced strawberries

Directions:

In a blender, combine the banana, avocado, kiwi, ginger, spinach, cinnamon, cashew butter, coconut milk, and maple syrup. Blend until thick, scraping down the sides of the blender when needed. Once blended, add spirulina and blend again until mixed. Pour into two bowls. Top the bowls with flaxseed, kiwi, and strawberry slices. You can drizzle with honey or maple syrup if desired.

Raspberry Sunrise Bowl

Ingredients:

- 1 cup gluten-free oats
- 1 cup coconut or almond milk
- pinch of sea salt
- 1 TBSP flax seeds
- 1 TBSP almond butter
- ⅓ – ¼ cup orange juice
- 1 TBSP coconut oil
- 1-2 TBSP maple syrup
- pinch nutmeg
- pinch ground ginger
- ¼ tsp salt
- 1 cup fresh berries
- sliced oranges
- crushed nuts
- 2oz coconut cream or dairy-free coconut yogurt

Directions:

In a microwave safe bowl, microwave the gluten-free oats, milk, salt and chia seeds and set aside. For stovetop, put those same ingredients in a small saucepan and cook on medium for 10 mins. Add optional almond butter for a creamier consistency. To make fruit compote, combine orange juice, coconut oil and maple syrup in a small saucepan over low heat. Add nutmeg, ginger, cinnamon, and berries. Bring to a soft boil for 1-2 minutes or until fruit is soft enough to mash. Divide between 2 bowls and spoon fruit compote over each bowl. Top with desired toppings.

Satisfying Chia Seed Pudding

Ingredients:

- ¼ cup chia seeds
- ¼ coconut milk (canned)
- ½ cup almond milk
- 1 TBSP raw honey
- 1 tsp pure vanilla
- 1 tsp cinnamon
- Toppings- banana, cranberries, coconut, raspberries, strawberries or any you like

Directions:

Mix coconut milk, almond milk, honey, vanilla, and cinnamon in a bowl and refrigerate overnight. In the morning stir and top with desired toppings.

Superfoods Breakfast Cookie

Ingredients:

- 1 cup gluten-free rolled oats
- ½ cup oat flour
- ½ cup dried cranberries
- ½ cup unsalted pumpkin seeds (pepitas)
- ¼ cup ground flaxseed
- 1 TBSP chia seeds
- 1 tsp cinnamon

- ½ tsp baking powder
- ¼ tsp salt
- 1 large organic mashed banana
- 3 TBSP melted coconut oil
- 3 TBSP honey
- 2 TBSP almond milk

Directions:

Preheat oven to 325°F. Combine dry ingredients in a large mixing bowl—oats, oat flour, dried cranberries, pumpkin seeds, ground flaxseed, chia seeds, cinnamon, baking powder, and salt.

Stir in mashed banana, coconut oil, and almond milk until well blended. Let mixture rest for 4–5 minutes, giving time for chia and flax to bind everything together. It should look like the dough. If your dough has gotten too thick, stir in an additional 1–2 TBSP milk before scooping out onto your baking sheet.

Measure dough out by the scant ¼ cupful and place on a baking sheet lined with parchment paper (or lightly greased). These cookies don't spread much while baking, so I like to gently press the dough with the palm of my hand to flatten a bit.

Bake for 15–18 minutes, or until cookies are lightly golden around the edges.

Yummy Breakfast Casserole

Ingredients:

- 12 large eggs
- 2 cups of cheese sharp or cheddar cheese
- 2 cups of canned coconut milk
- 1 tsp salt
- pepper to taste

Favorite Toppings:
- Sautéed mushrooms
- Steamed asparagus
- Diced tomatoes
- Cooked turkey sausage
- Optional top with green onions once cooked

Directions:

Combine all ingredients except cheese in a mixing bowl and beat well. Pour mixture into a greased 9×13-inch glass or ceramic pan. Then place cheese and your favorite toppings (see above) on top. Take a fork and lightly push them into the egg mixture. Bake at 350°F for 30-40 minutes until the casserole is browned and a knife comes out clean.

Cherries and Berries Smoothie

Ingredients:

- 1 cup frozen cherries
- ½ cup frozen raspberries
- ½ cup frozen spinach
- 2 tsp Maca root powder (can be found on Amazon, or health food stores)
- 1 TBSP no sugar added almond butter
- 1 tsp pure vanilla extract
- 1-inch piece of ginger root or a dash of ground ginger
- 1 scoop unsweetened pea or rice protein powder (NutriBiotic rice protein is my favorite)
- ½ TBSP of almond butter
- 1 cup filtered water or nut milk of choice (unsweetened vanilla almond is my favorite)
- a few ice cubes

Directions:

Blend all ingredients in a Nutri Ninja/blender until smooth.

Serve in a pretty glass with a straw.

Strawberry Dream Smoothie

Ingredients:

- 1 cup frozen strawberries
- ½ cup frozen blueberries
- ½ frozen Avocado
- ½ cup frozen spinach
- 1 tsp maca root powder (amazon or any health food store)
- 1 scoop pea or rice protein powder (amazon or any health food store)
- ½ TBSP almond or coconut butter
- 1 tsp vanilla
- 1 tsp cinnamon
- 1 tsp ground ginger
- 1 cup milk of choice (unsweetened vanilla almond is my favorite)

Directions:

Blend until smooth in a Nutri Ninja or blender

Serve in a pretty glass with a straw.

Overnight Oats

Ingredients:

- 1 cup gluten-free whole-grain oats (favorite is Bob's red mill)
- ½ cup of full-fat plain Greek yogurt
- 1 TBSP ground flax seeds
- 1 TBSP chia seeds
- 1 scoop pea or rice protein powder
- 1 cup almond milk or nut milk of choice
- Top with a sprinkle of a nut of choice and ½ TBSP nut butter of choice (choose low sugar such as Justin's)
- Top with blueberries or strawberries

Directions:

Mix all ingredients except toppings in a bowl. Divide between 2 jars and top with 1 TBSP of nuts and 1 TBSP nut butter. Put in fridge overnight, and in the morning top with blueberries or strawberries. Enjoy!

Yield 2 servings

Whole grains are plant foods that include all parts of the grain kernel: the bran, germ and endosperm. Whole grains contain the most nutrients including B vitamins, magnesium, chromium and fiber. They are the best source of complex "slow" carbohydrates as they are high in fiber, enzymes, antioxidants, vitamins and minerals.

Sweet Potato Avocado Toast

Ingredients:

- 1-2 sweet potatoes sliced long ways and ½" thick
- Almond butter
- Walnuts
- Avocado
- Chia seeds
- Coldwater salmon/lox
- Banana
- Hummus
- Sea salt
- Red onion

Foods rich in Vitamin B6 such as sweet potatoes and bananas are important for hormone regulation and regularity of menstrual cycles.

Essential fatty acids such as coldwater fish and flax seeds are highly recommended because they combat cellular inflammation and improve hormonal sensitivity.

Stay away from trans fats because they are a powerful deterrent to ovulation and conception.

Directions:

Toast sweet potato for 2-3 cycles until just soft enough to eat but not mushy and pick 2 varieties or create your own.

Top with 1 TBSP nut butter, 1 tsp chia seeds and walnuts

Top with 1 TBSP hummus, ½ avocado/sliced, and 1 tsp sea salt

Top with ½ cup lox and sliced red onion

Top with 1 TBSP nut butter, 1 TBSP walnuts, and 1 tsp chia seeds

Yield 5 servings

Almond Flour Pancakes

Ingredients:

- 1 cup almond flour
- 1 cup nut milk
- 3 flax eggs (1 TBSP water, 1 TBSP flax seeds, let sit 5 mins)
- ¼ tsp sea salt
- 2 tsp baking powder
- 1 tsp baking soda
- ¼ cup olive, grapeseed or avocado oil

Directions:

Add almond flour and nut milk to a blender or food processor and blend on high for 3 minutes

Add remaining ingredients and blend until smooth

Cook on a hot griddle for 1-2 minutes on each side or until golden (batter will be very thin).

This is normal. Trust this and treat it like a regular pancake.

When you see the bubbles, flip.

Top with blackberries, blueberries or cherries with coconut cream.

Coconut cream -

Use full-fat coconut milk in a can. Put can in the fridge overnight. In the morning, open can and scoop out the solid. Add 1 TBSP pure vanilla and beat until creamy. Keeps in the fridge for 1 week.

Yield 10-12 servings

Yummy in my Tummy Granola

Ingredients:

- ⅓ cup creamy all-natural almond butter
- ½ cup walnuts
- ¼ cup almonds
- ½ cup pumpkin seeds
- ⅓ cup coconut oil
- 1 heaping tsp pure vanilla extract
- ½ tsp ground cinnamon
- 2 ½ cups quinoa
- OR 2 ½ cups gluten-free oats

Directions:

Preheat oven to 300°F.

Line a baking sheet with parchment paper and set aside.

Mix almond butter and melted coconut oil in a medium bowl, until smooth

Stir in vanilla and cinnamon until well incorporated. Add dry ingredients and stir until they are well coated.

Spread mixture onto parchment paper in an even layer.

Bake at 300 for 30 minutes total, flipping the pieces over after 15-20 minutes.

This helps it get crunchy all over. If you flip carefully and leave lots of it stuck together, you'll get huge clusters.

Let cool completely to firm up. (It can be soft out of the oven, but it does get hard and crunchy as it cools.) Store in an airtight container for up to 3 weeks and enjoy!

Yield 10 servings

Lunch

Roasted Veggies and Protein

Ingredients:

- ¼ cup cooked quinoa
- ½ cup bone broth (homemade)
- 2 medium organic carrots sliced lengthwise
- 1 medium organic zucchini sliced in thin rounds
- 1 handful of organic broccoli florets
- 1 handful of organic cauliflower
- 1 medium organic sweet potato sliced in rounds
- 1 egg
- 1 TBSP pumpkin seeds
- 1 TBSP sunflower seeds
- 1 TBSP feta or blue cheese
- 1 sprinkle of cherry tomatoes
- ½ sliced organic avocado
- 1 TBSP organic dried cranberries
- 1-2 TBSP organic grapeseed or avocado oil
- 1 TBSP cinnamon
- ½ tsp pink Himalayan sea salt

Dressing:
- 5 TBSP apple cider vinegar
- 4 TBSP olive oil
- 1-2 tsp pure maple syrup
- 1-2 tsp brown mustard
- 1 tsp pink Himalayan salt
- 1 tsp organic minced garlic

Directions:

Place all veggies in a freezer bag with grapeseed or avocado oil, cinnamon, and sea salt and shake a few times to coat veggies. Roast veggies on a sheet pan at 450 for 20 mins. Fry egg (omit if vegan). Layer quinoa, 1–2 cups veggies, seeds, avocado, tomatoes, cheese. (omit the cheese if vegan). Place fried egg on top. Put 1-2 TBSP dressing on and enjoy.

Estrogen reducing and B12 containing foods such as broccoli, cauliflower, and cheese help prevent estrogen dominance which disrupts the thyroid hormone conversion (T4 and T3) which can affect your ability to conceive, lose or gain weight or feel your best. B12 deficiency and abnormal estrogen levels may interfere with implantation of the fertilized egg. B12 also strengthens the endometrium lining in egg fertilization, decreasing the risk of miscarriage.

Corn and Black Bean Jar Salad

Ingredients:

- 1 cup dry quinoa, rinsed and cooked
- 1 (15 oz) can black beans, drained and rinsed
- 1-pint cherry tomatoes, halved
- 2 bell peppers, cored and diced
- 1 cup corn kernels
- 3 green onions, diced
- diced avocado for serving (optional)

Cumin-Lime Dressing
- 1 cup cilantro
- ½ cup lime juice (approx.. 4 limes)
- 2 garlic cloves
- 1-2 jalapenos, depending on size
- 2 tsp cumin
- ½ tsp chili powder
- ½ tsp salt
- 2 TBSP extra virgin olive oil

Directions:

Cook quinoa per package.

Meanwhile, make the dressing by adding all the ingredients to a food processor or blender and blending until smooth.

Once the quinoa has cooled, divide it evenly between 4 (16 oz) jars. Pour a quarter of the dressing into each jar and gently stir to combine. Next layer the black beans, corn, bell pepper, green onion and tomato on top. Seal with a lid and refrigerate for up to 4 days. When ready to serve, dump the salad out into a bowl and top with diced avocado.

Yield 4 servings

Superfoods Green Salad

Ingredients:

- 2 cups organic broccoli
- 1 cup organic kale
- 1 yellow organic pear
- 1 cup organic red cabbage
- 1 cup organic carrots
- 1-1/2 cups fresh parsley
- 1 organic cucumber
- ½ cup almonds
- ½ cup sunflower seeds (unsalted)
- ⅓ cup organic craisins

For the Vinaigrette
- 3 TBSP olive oil
- ½ cup lemon juice
- 1 TBSP fresh ginger, peeled and grated
- 1 TBSP coconut oil
- ½ tsp sea salt

Directions:

Either chop the ingredients using a good sharp knife or toss them individually in a food processor and quickly process until they're finely chopped.

Place the ingredients for the vinaigrette in a jar with a lid. Place the lid on the jar and shake the ingredients. Or place all the ingredients in a small bowl and whisk to incorporate well.

Add all the salad ingredients to a large bowl and toss with the vinaigrette.

Healthy Taco Bowl

Ingredients:

- ¾ cup cooked quinoa
- ⅛ tsp salt
- zest of 1 lime
- ¾ lb lean ground turkey
- 2 TBSP of my taco seasoning (recipe in this book)
- ½ cup white mushrooms

- ¼ cup red onion minced
- juice from ½ a lime
- ⅛ tsp salt
- 1 can black beans
- 1 avocado
- 1 egg hardboiled (optional)
- ¼ cup nutritional yeast (vegan)

Directions:

Cook Quinoa according to package directions, adding the lime zest and salt to the cooking water.

Cook turkey over medium heat, tossing in the taco seasoning and breaking it up as you cook. Cook for 10 or so minutes, until cooked through.

To assemble bowls:

- ¼ portion of cooked quinoa (roughly ½ cup)
- ½ cup cooked taco meat
- ½ cup sautéed white mushrooms (cook in a little coconut oil for sweet flavor)
- ¼ cup red onion
- ¼ cup black beans
- ¼ cup avocado diced
- 1-2 TBSP nutritional yeast

BBQ Chickpea Wrap with Homemade Ranch

Ingredients:

- ⅓ cup BBQ chickpeas
- 1 cup lettuce
- 1 roma tomato, finely chopped
- ½ lime
- 1 lettuce leaf or gluten-free wrap
- 2 ½ TBSP ranch dressing

Directions:

BBQ Chickpeas in a small pot over medium heat, place 1, 15oz can of chickpeas and 2 TBSP homemade barbecue sauce. Heat for about 5 minutes until warm and the sauce becomes sticky and coats the chickpeas.

Remove from the heat and coat with the remaining barbecue sauce. If desired, you can add more barbecue sauce.

Heat ½ tsp olive oil or coconut oil in a skillet over medium heat (if possible, brush with a pastry brush).

Place a wrap in the heat for about 30 seconds on each side to heat up. Or, microwave the wrap for about 15 to 30 seconds. Set on a plate to assemble. or use a lettuce leaf for carb-free.

Layer with BBQ chickpeas, lettuce, tomato, and ranch dressing, then squeeze the juice of the lime over it all. Wrap up, cut in half, and enjoy! You can also serve the ranch dressing on the side.

Homemade Ranch

Ingredients:

- 1 cup mayonnaise or veganaise
- ½ cup sour cream or coconut yogurt
- ½ cup buttermilk
- ½ cup fresh parsley finely chopped
- 2 cloves garlic minced
- 1 green onion finely chopped
- 1 TBSP fresh dill
- ½ tsp salt
- ¼ tsp black pepper
- dash paprika

Directions:

Whisk mayonnaise and sour cream together, then whisk in buttermilk.

Mix in parsley, garlic, green onion, dill, salt, pepper, and paprika.

Cover and refrigerate at least 2 hours or overnight.

Homemade BBQ Sauce

Ingredients:

- 1 can tomato sauce (15 oz)
- 1 can tomato paste (6 oz)
- ⅓ cup apple cider vinegar
- ¼ cup pure maple syrup
- ¼ cup molasses
- 2 TBSP Worcestershire sauce
- 2 tsp smoked paprika
- 1 tsp dry mustard
- 1 tsp garlic powder
- ½ tsp kosher salt
- ½ tsp black pepper
- ⅛ – ¼ tsp cayenne pepper —optional

Directions:

In a medium saucepan, stir together all the ingredients: tomato sauce, tomato paste, apple cider vinegar, maple syrup, molasses, Worcestershire, smoked paprika, dry mustard, garlic, salt, black pepper, and cayenne pepper. Bring to a simmer over medium heat. Cover with a lid slightly ajar so that the pot is mostly covered to deter splattering, but steam can still escape, and the sauce can reduce. Let cook, stirring occasionally, until the sauce thickens, about 10 to 15 minutes, Taste and adjust seasonings as desired. Enjoy immediately or let cool and store in an airtight container in the refrigerator for up to 1 week.

Tomato Quinoa + Roasted Veggies

Ingredients:

- 1 TBSP olive oil
- ½ cup cherry tomatoes
- 2 red peppers
- 1 large zucchini
- A generous pinch of salt and pepper

For the quinoa
- 1 TBSP olive oil
- 1 large red onion, diced
- 3 garlic cloves, minced

- 1 cup of quinoa
- 1 TBSP balsamic vinegar
- 1 cup vegetable stock
- Approximately 6 sun-dried tomatoes, chopped into small chunks
- A small bunch of fresh basil, torn
- salt and pepper, to taste
- Optional nutritional yeast to serve

Directions:

Preheat the oven to 350°F and add the olive oil to a roasting tin.

Chop the vegetables into small chunks and spread out in the tin, adding the salt and pepper before giving everything a shake to coat.

Roast for 30 minutes.

To make the risotto:

Meanwhile, add olive oil to a shallow casserole dish or large frying pan, on low-medium heat. Sauté the onion for a few minutes before adding the minced garlic and cooking for another minute.

Stir in the quinoa with the vinegar and stir for approximately 30 seconds, to coat it in the oil. Pour in the vegetable stock, 1/2 cup at a time, alternating between the two. Allow each amount to be absorbed by the quinoa before adding the next.

After 20 minutes, add in the sun-dried tomatoes and the roasted vegetables. Stir everything, adding more liquid if needed, and cook for a further 5 minutes until everything is cooked through and the quinoa is done.

Remove from the heat and stir in the basil, salt and pepper, and vegan cheese (if using). Feel free to stir in any extra oil or dairy-free butter at this point for an extra creamy risotto.

Serve right away and enjoy!

Fish Tacos

Ingredients:

- 8-12 oz firm white fish (halibut or cod)
- ½ cup coconut milk
- ¾ cup shredded coconut flakes
- ½ cup gluten-free bread crumbs
- 1 TBSP curry powder
- 1 TBSP cumin
- 1 tsp sea salt
- 4 Romaine lettuce leaves

Mango salsa
- 1 ripe mango peeled and diced into 4-inch cubes
- ⅛ cup cilantro, roughly chopped
- ½ cup diced tomatoes
- ¼ cup diced jalapeno pepper
- 2 tsp grated ginger root (peeled)
- Fresh squeezed juice and zest from 1 lime
- ½ Avocado, diced
- 4 red onion, chopped

Directions:

4 large romaine lettuce leaves (as shells) Skin fish and cut into ½ inch thick slices. Dunk each piece in the coconut milk, then into the curry-coconut mixture. Coat on all sides. Cook each fish in coconut oil over medium heat until both sides are brown. Make mango salsa by combining all ingredients.

To serve- Lay out 4 lettuce leaves. Fill each with cooked fish and top with salsa, avocado slices, and red onion.

Yummy Jar Salad

Ingredients:

- 1 cup all-natural diced chicken
- 1 avocado, diced
- ½ cup beets, sliced thin
- 1 small clove Garlic, minced
- 2 cup spinach
- 1 cucumber, chopped

- 1-2 TBSP nutritional yeast
- 1/2 TBSP Lemon juice
- 1 sprinkle each Salt & pepper
- 1 ½ TBSP extra virgin olive oil
- 1 TBSP apple cider vinegar

Directions:

Mix the olive oil, vinegar, lemon juice, and garlic in a small bowl. Season with salt and pepper. Set aside.

Steam, sauté or roast chicken and cube. Chop the beets, spinach, cucumber and lettuce.

Arrange the mason jar salad by adding the dressing to the bottom of the jar first (about 2 TBSP each jar)

Add:

- 1 cup of spinach
- ½ cup beets
- ¼ cup cucumber

- ½ cup chicken
- Avocado -chopped
- Top with nutritional yeast, if using.

Seal and store in the fridge for up to 3 days. Shake or pour the salad into a bowl when ready to eat. Add avocado at the end so it doesn't brown before eating.

Yield 1-2 servings

Soup

Creamy Tomato Soup

Ingredients:

- 2 TBSP oil or cooking fat of choice
- 1 large onion, peeled and chopped
- 4 garlic cloves, peeled and chopped
- 1 can (28oz) crushed, diced and whole peeled tomatoes
- 1 ½ cups chicken or veggie stock
- 1 cup unsweetened coconut milk
- 2 TBSP minced fresh basil, plus 1 TBSP for garnish
- 1 TBSP tomato paste
- 1 TBSP balsamic vinegar

Tomatoes are progesterone promoting. And soup warms the soul.

Directions:

In a large Dutch oven or soup pot that is already hot, heat the oil over medium heat. Add the onions, and sauté until just about translucent, about 4 minutes. Stir in the garlic and sauté for 1 minute more. Mix in the remaining ingredients, and simmer for 5 to 10 minutes to allow the flavors to meld, or cook everything except coconut milk on low for 3 hours. 30 minutes before ready to serve, add coconut milk and cook 30 minutes more. Carefully pour one or two cups of the soup mixture into a blender (until it is only half full) and puree until smooth.

Remove to a separate soup pot or container, and repeat with the remaining soup mixture, working in batches. Alternatively, you can use an immersion blender to puree the soup mixture. Serve hot, topped with some minced basil for garnish.

Adzuki Bean Soup

Ingredients:

- 1 ½ cups adzuki beans, wash then put in a large bowl, cover with water & leave to soak overnight (or 6-8 hours)
- 2 bay leaves
- 1 cup pumpkin or butternut squash cut into 2" cubes
- salt & black pepper
- 4 ½ cups veggie stock
- 2 large carrots, chopped
- 2 TBSP white miso paste
- 1 TBSP curry powder
- a big handful of fresh parsley or coriander, finely chopped

Directions:

Put all the ingredients except the miso and herbs in a crockpot and cook on low for 6-8 hours.

In the last 30 minutes, dissolve the miso paste in a cup with a small amount of the hot broth and then add to the pot. Simmer for 1 more minute then turn off the heat. Stir in the fresh herbs, and taste to check seasoning.

Serve in warmed bowls garnished with extra fresh herbs.

Yield 6-8 servings

Hormone Balancing Bean Soup

Ingredients:

- 1 cup dried lentils
- 6 cups filtered water
- 1 medium onion, diced
- 2 garlic cloves
- 1 carrot, sliced diagonally
- 1 parsnip, sliced diagonally
- 1 sweet potato
- 1 cup kale, loosely chopped
- 1 TBSP pumpkin seeds
- ½ avocado

According to fertility expert, Heather Rodriguez, women who do not get enough iron may suffer lack of ovulation and possibly poor egg health, which can inhibit pregnancy at a rate of 60%. Eating beans on a regular basis is a great way to get iron, vitamin E, and folate acid.

Directions:

Place all ingredients in a crockpot and cook on low for 6-8 hours. Garnish with goat cheese crumbles, pumpkin seeds, and diced avocado.

Soothing Black Bean Soup

Ingredients:

- 2 cloves garlic
- 1 medium organic onion
- 2 medium organic carrots
- 1 lb dry uncooked black beans or 3 cans of organic black beans
- 1 cup salsa
- 1 can organic diced tomatoes
- 1 bunch organic kale
- 1 TBSP chili powder
- ½ TBSP cumin
- 1 tsp oregano
- 4 cups vegetable broth

Toppings
- Feta, sour cream, cilantro

Directions:

Dice the onion and chop the carrots

Combine the garlic, onion, carrots, black beans, chili powder, cumin, oregano, vegetable broth, and water in a 5-7-quart slow cooker. Stir well.

Place the lid on the slow cooker and cook on low (canned beans), or high (dry beans) for 6-8 hours. In the last hour add the salsa. In the last 15 minutes add 1 cup kale.

Thai Squash Stew

Ingredients:

- 1 small butternut squash cubed
- 1 cup kale
- 1 TBSP coconut oil
- ¾ cup onions chopped
- 3 TBSP celery chopped
- 1½ tsp ginger grated
- 2 TBSP Thai red curry paste
- 1 TBSP curry powder
- Salt to taste
- 1 tsp fish sauce

- 2 tsp brown sugar
- ¾ cup vegetable stock
- 1 cup canned coconut milk
- Handful basil leaves roughly torn

For garnish –

- Roasted and crushed peanuts
- Roasted cashews
- Fresh coriander leaves
- Lime wedges

Directions:

Add all ingredients except coconut milk, fish sauce, sugar and kale to a crockpot. Cook on low for 6-8 hours.

Once cooked and squash is soft add the remaining ingredients and cook 30 minutes more. Tear kale and stir in.

Tear basil leaves and sprinkle it over the curry. Served with hot rice (jasmine or brown rice) or quinoa.

White Bean Chicken Chili

Ingredients:

- 1 ¼ lb of boneless, skinless organic chicken (2-3 breasts)
- 4 cups low-sodium chicken broth
- 2 (15 oz cans) reduced-sodium great northern beans rinsed and drained
- 2 (4 ½ oz) cans diced green chilis
- 3 garlic cloves
- 1 small yellow onion, finely diced
- 2 tsp ground cumin
- 1 tsp dried oregano
- ½ tsp kosher salt
- ¼ tsp cayenne pepper
- ¼ cup chopped fresh cilantro
- Fresh lime wedges
- Toppings- diced jalapeños, diced avocado, sour cream, shredded cheese, nutritional yeast

Directions:

Place chicken in the bottom of a 6 quart or larger slow cooker. Top with chicken broth, white beans, green chilies, garlic, onion, cumin, oregano, salt, and cayenne. Stir to combine. Cover and cook on low for 4-6 hours until the chicken is cooked through. Remove the chicken breasts and transfer them to a plate.

Once cool enough to handle, shred and add back to the soup. Stir in cilantro. Portion into bowls and top with a squeeze of fresh lime juice. Add desired toppings.

Yield 6-8 servings

Bone Broth

Ingredients:

- 5-10 grass-fed beef bones
- 2-4 TBSP organic apple cider vinegar
- 1-2 bay leaves
- 1 white or yellow onion
- 2 carrots
- 6 cups filtered water

Bone broth has so many amazing qualities for balancing hormones and fighting infertility. The main one is, it regulates your gut microbiome which controls every aspect of the body from immune health, hormones and your endocrine system, brain health, fuels hair, skin and nail growth and tastes delicious. You can also give it to your babies as their first meal.

Directions:

Place bones and apple cider vinegar in crockpot or Instapot let sit for 1-2 hours.

Put in bay leaf, onion, and carrots and fill to fill line with filtered water.

Pressure cook on high for 4-5 hours and set it to natural release. Let it sit in the pot until cool, and then place it in jars in the fridge. When ready to eat, cut the fat off the top, but leave a little in the pan along with the liquid. Heat until warm and enjoy.

For crockpot – put in the same ingredients and cook for 6-8 hours.

Same jarring instructions as above.

For stovetop – simmer for 24-48 hours, test a little by putting a small amount in the fridge. If it turns to gel it is ready, if not, simmer it longer. Cool slightly and then jar.

Bone Broth Brussel Sprouts

Ingredients:

- 2 lbs of halved brussels sprouts
- ¼ cup organic chicken or beef bone broth
- 5-6 slices organic bacon, chopped
- 2 TBSP melted ghee
- ½ tsp sea salt

Directions:

Preheat oven to 450°F and line a baking sheet with parchment paper

Heat a large skillet over medium-high heat.

Add brussels sprouts and bone broth and gently sauté until brussels sprouts turn bright green, about 4-5 minutes.

Carefully transfer the Brussels to the lined baking sheet. Drizzle with melted ghee, sprinkle with sea salt and ½ the chopped bacon.

Roast for 25-30 minutes until crispy and top with the other ½ of the chopped bacon.

Enjoy.

Brussel sprouts and bone broth are a great way to get lots of healthy vitamins, collagen and connective tissues into your diet.

Dinner

Spicy Vegan Chili

Ingredients:

- 2 TBSP olive oil
- 1 medium onion, chopped
- 1 med green, red and yellow pepper, seeded and chopped
- 1 jalapeno pepper, seeded and chopped
- 4 cloves garlic, minced
- 1 cup vegetable broth
- 1 can crushed tomatoes (32 oz)
- 1 can black beans (14 oz), drained and rinsed
- 1 TBSP ground cumin
- 1 TBSP ground chili powder
- 6 dashes hot sauce or tabasco sauce
- coarse salt to taste
- 1 cup spicy vegetarian re-fried beans
- ½ avocado

Directions:

Heat the oil in a deep pot over medium-high heat. Add the onion, peppers and sauce, stirring frequently for 5-8 minutes. Add garlic and cook 1 minute more. Add broth and then scrape up any good stuff from the bottom of the pan. Reduce the liquid by half, cooking it down for 2 or 3 minutes. Add the tomatoes and beans, and season with cumin, chili powder, hot sauce, and salt. Simmer for 15 minutes. Thicken by stirring in re-fried beans and cook for 5 minutes more.

Quinoa Crust Easy Pizza

Ingredients:

For the Crust:

- ¾ cup quinoa covered by 1" of water, soaked for 6-8 hours (or overnight)
- ¼ cup water
- ½ tsp baking powder
- ½ tsp salt
- 2 TBSP olive oil

Optional Toppings:

- ½ cup tomato sauce
- Goat cheese balls or shredded
- Red pepper flakes
- 1 cup shredded nutritional yeast
- Fresh herbs including basil

Directions:

Soak the quinoa in water, covering it by at least 1 inch, for 6-8 hours.

Once you're ready to make the crust, preheat oven to 425°F. Line a 9-inch cake pan with parchment paper and drizzle one TBSP of oil in the center. Spread around with your hands until evenly coated and set pan aside.

Thoroughly rinse quinoa, then add to a blender. Add the ¼ cup of water, baking powder, salt and remaining olive oil, and blend on high until smooth and creamy. This should resemble a thick pancake batter.

Pour batter into prepared pan and bake for 15 minutes. Remove, flip and return to oven baking for another 10–15 minutes until browned and edges are crispy.

Top with sauce, cheese and any other toppings you'd like and bake for 12-15 minutes until cheese has melted and started to brown.

Remove, let it cool for a few minutes in the pan, then transfer it to a cutting board and slice.

Garnish with herbs, nutritional yeast, etc., and serve immediately!

Yields 4-6 Servings

Thai Veggie Quinoa Bowls

Ingredients:

- ½ cup broccoli finely diced
- ½ cup quinoa cooked according to package directions
- ½ small red onion diced
- ¼ cup grated carrots
- handful cilantro chopped
- ¼ cup chopped green onions
- 2 TBSP almonds chopped

For the Dressing:

- 1 lime zest and juice (start with juice from half a lime, and add more if needed)
- 1 tsp sesame seeds
- 1 TBSP gluten-free tamari
- 1 TBSP sesame oil
- 1 TBSP rice vinegar
- 2 cloves garlic minced
- 1-inch piece of ginger minced

Directions:

In a large bowl, toss together the cooked quinoa, broccoli, red onion, carrots, cilantro, green onions, and almonds.

Mix until combined.

In a small bowl combine dressing ingredients.

Pour dressing over the quinoa and mix until combined. You can also roast your veggies first if you don't want them raw.

Sweet Potato + Black Bean Enchiladas

Ingredients:

Filling:
- 1 ¼ lb sweet potatoes (2 small-to-medium)
- 1 can (15 oz) black beans, rinsed and drained, or cooked black beans
- 4 oz (1 cup) grated Monterey Jack cheese
- 2 oz (½ cup) crumbled feta cheese
- 2 small cans (4 oz each) diced green chilis
- 1 medium jalapeño, seeded and minced
- 2 cloves garlic, pressed or minced
- 2 TBSP lime juice
- ½ tsp ground cumin
- ½ tsp chili powder
- ¼ tsp cayenne pepper (optional)
- ¼ tsp salt, to taste
- Freshly ground black pepper

Remaining Ingredients
- 2 cups (16 oz) mild salsa verde
- 10 corn tortillas
- 4 oz (1 cup) grated Monterey Jack cheese
- 2 TBSP sour cream
- 1 TBSP water
- ¼ cup chopped red onion
- ¼ cup chopped fresh cilantro

Directions:

Pre-heat oven to 400°F and cook sweet potatoes in the oven until soft and easy to scoop out. Cover the bottom of a 9×13-inch baking dish with salsa verde. In a medium mixing bowl, combine all the remaining filling ingredients.

Scoop out the insides of the sweet potatoes, and season them to taste with additional salt (I added ¼ tsp) and pepper.

Warm up your tortillas, one by one in a skillet when you bend them. Wrap them in a tea towel so they stay warm. Working with one tortilla at a time, spread about ½ cup filling down the middle of each tortilla, then wrap both sides over the filling and place it in your baking dish.

Repeat for all the tortillas.

Top with the remaining salsa verde, and cheese. Bake for 25 to 35 minutes, until the sauce is bubbling, and the cheese is lightly golden.

Let the enchiladas cool for about 5 minutes. Whisk the sour cream and water together to make a drizzly sour cream sauce. Drizzle it back and forth over the enchiladas, then top them with cilantro and red onion. Serve.

Polenta with Roasted Vegetables

Ingredients:

- 2 organic sweet potatoes chopped into ½ inch pieces
- 1 cup polenta
- 2 organic carrots chopped
- ½ cup organic broccoli
- 1-pint grape or cherry tomatoes, halved
- 3 small or 2 medium-sized zucchinis, cut into 1-inch chunks
- ½ red onion, thinly sliced
- 2 TBSP extra-virgin olive oil

- Kosher salt
- 2 garlic cloves, finely chopped
- ½ tsp crushed red chili flakes
- 2 tsp chopped fresh thyme or rosemary
- 1 TBSP balsamic vinegar
- 1 cup coarse cornmeal
- 1–2 tsp salt
- ½ cup grated fresh Parmesan cheese
- 4 TBSP butter

Directions:

Preheat the oven to 425°F.

Put all veggies in a zip-lock bag with ½ tsp of salt, and 1 TBSP of olive oil, shake, then place on pan and roast until beginning to soften and turn brown, 20-25 minutes. Remove the pan from the oven and stir in the garlic, thyme and balsamic vinegar.

Meanwhile, bring 4 cups of water to a boil in a heavy-duty saucepan or small Dutch oven. Stir in 1 tsp salt. Gradually sprinkle the cornmeal into the pan while whisking at the same time. Turn the heat to a very low simmer, add 1 cup of polenta, cover and continue to cook the polenta for 25-30 minutes, until it's thick, fluffy and begins to pull away from the sides of the pan. Stir occasionally so it doesn't stick to the bottom of the pan. When it's done remove from the heat and stir in the cheese, butter, and additional salt to taste if needed.

Serve the warm polenta in bowls with the roasted vegetables and their juices over the top; sprinkle with additional cheese if you like.

Veggie Quesadillas

Ingredients:

- 4 medium flour tortillas
- 1 large sweet potato
- 2 avocados
- ½ cup black beans rinsed and Drained
- ¼ cup corn rinsed and drained
- 1 mini red pepper
- 1 mini orange pepper
- 1 tsp Jalapeno diced-optional
- 1 TBSP easy homemade taco seasoning
- 1 cup cheddar or pepper jack cheese
- 1 TBSP coconut oil
- 2 tsp olive oil, divided

Directions:

Prepare Filling.

Use a fork to poke several holes into the sweet potato and drizzle with 1 tsp olive oil. You can also sprinkle with a small amount of salt and pepper. Wrap the sweet potato in paper towels and microwave for 8 minutes or until very tender. Or roast in the oven until soft, about 50-60 minutes.

Dice jalapeno and peppers removing the ribs and seeds. Add diced peppers and jalapeno (if using) to a large pan and cook until tender, about 5-7 minutes. Then add black beans, corn, and taco seasoning and stir to combine cooking another 3 minutes. Pour into a bowl and set aside.

Assemble the Quesadilla.

Lightly spread butter over one side of the tortilla. On the other side spread about 3 TBSP of sweet potato over the tortilla. Next mash half of an avocado over the sweet potato. Add about ¼ cup of the veggie/bean filling over the top of the avocado. Finally, sprinkle a generous amount of cheese over top.

Place the butter side of the tortilla down on the warm pan and cook over medium heat until the tortilla is browned, and cheese is melted. Carefully fold the tortilla in half on to itself using the spatula. Repeat until all tortillas are filled and cooked. Slice and serve warm with suggested toppings and enjoy!

Coconut Lime Chicken

Ingredients:

- 1 shallot, diced
- 4 cloves of garlic, minced
- 1 TBSP fresh ginger, grated
- ¼ cup fresh cilantro, chopped (plus more for topping)
- ⅓ cup lime juice (about 2 limes)

- 4 organic chicken breasts
- 2 TBSP avocado oil (or coconut oil)
- ¼ cup chicken broth
- 1½ cups full-fat coconut milk
- salt and pepper
- lime slices (optional)

Directions:

Prep shallot, garlic, ginger and cilantro as noted. Juice limes and set aside.

Place the chicken breasts between two pieces of parchment paper and pound them down to make them even in thickness. Sprinkle each side of the chicken with salt and pepper.

Heat a large skillet over medium heat and add avocado oil.

Once hot, add the chicken to the pan (you may have to cook the chicken in 2 batches depending on the size of your pan). Cook, without disturbing for 3-4 minutes, until a nice brown crust has formed. Flip and cook another 3-4 minutes on the other side, until the chicken is mostly cooked through. Remove chicken from the skillet and set aside. Lower the heat to medium.

Add more oil if needed and add the garlic and shallot to the pan. Cook, stirring constantly, for 1-2 minutes.

Add chicken stock, coconut milk, lime juice, ginger and cilantro to the pan. Stir to mix, scraping up any browned bits remaining in the pan from when you cooked your chicken.

Add the chicken breasts back to the skillet with the sauce. Cover and turn the heat down to low. Simmer for 5 minutes, or until the chicken is fully cooked.

Serve with vegetables, potatoes, rice or cauliflower rice. Spoon some sauce over everything for serving. Sprinkle with cilantro and garnish with lime slices (optional).

Roasted Squash and Feta Couscous

Ingredients:

- 1 TBSP olive or rapeseed oil
- 1 butternut squash – peeled and chopped into bite-sized pieces
- 1 red onion – peeled and chopped into wedges
- 2 cloves of garlic – left whole in skin
- ¼ – ½ cup feta cheese – cubed
- 1 TBSP pine nuts (heaping)
- a handful of chopped basil
- 1 package of tomato flavored couscous

Directions:

Heat the oven to 400°F.

Toss the squash, onion, and garlic in the olive oil then spread into a roasting tin and roast for around 25 minutes or until everything is tender.

Once the squash is cooked – squeeze the skin off the garlic, and gently mix into the squash and onion.

Prepare the couscous as per the packet instructions and once cooked tip into the roasting tin.

Lightly toast the pine nuts in a dry frying pan – this takes around 1-2 minutes.

Add the nuts, feta, and basil to the couscous and vegetables, stir gently to mix everything together.

Divide between plates to serve.

Whole Crockpot Melt in your Mouth Chicken

Ingredients:

- 1 whole 4-6 lb chicken, giblets removed
- ½ tsp fresh black pepper
- ½ tsp fresh thyme (or 1 TBSP dried)
- 1 clove of garlic, minced
- 1 tsp onion powder
- 2 tsp paprika
- 2 tsp kosher salt

Directions:

Take the whole chicken and rinse it inside and out with water.

Pat dry and set aside.

Mix together all the seasonings in a small dish.

Using your fingers, gently lift the skin over the breasts by sliding your fingers up towards the neck to separate the skin and meat.

Rub the spice mixture all over the chicken, over the skin and underneath right onto the breast meat.

Place the chicken in a crock pot on low for 8 hours.

Once the chicken is done, remove from the crock pot and serve with a sweet potato and veggies. (can use bones to make broth)

Yield 6-8 servings

Sweet Chili Lime Salmon

Ingredients:

- ½ cup freshly squeezed lime juice (or juice of 2 limes)
- ¼ cup fresh chopped parsley
- 2 TBSP olive oil
- 2 TBSP Coconut oil
- 2 TBSP water
- 1 TBSP minced garlic (or 4 crushed garlic cloves)
- 1 tsp ground Cumin
- 1½ tsp salt
- 4 salmon fillets (wild-caught)
- 1 onion, cut into wedges
- 1 bunch of asparagus

Directions:

Preheat oven to 400°F. Spray a baking sheet with cooking oil spray; set aside.

Whisk lime juice, parsley, olive oil, water, garlic cumin, salt, and parsley together to combine. Add coconut oil and whisk again until it runs smooth through the rest of the ingredients.

Arrange the salmon fillets and onion in a single layer on the prepared baking tray and pour over half of the marinade.

Toss to coat and rotate the salmon to coat in the marinade.

Broil or grill until the onion is beginning to char at the edges (about 10 minutes) and the salmon is cooked to your liking (about 10 minutes).

Remove from the oven and serve immediately with lime wedges and remaining marinade for added flavor. Sauté asparagus in 1 TBSP olive oil with a little sea salt and pepper and top with a little nutritional yeast.

Yield 4 Servings

Grilled Yummy Baked Chicken

Ingredients:

- 4 boneless, skinless all-natural chicken breasts
- 2 TBSP grape seed/avocado oil
- 1 tsp sea salt
- ½ tsp crushed black pepper
- ½ tsp garlic powder
- ½ tsp onion powder
- ½ tsp chili powder

Directions:

Preheat oven to 450°F. Pound chicken breasts lightly so they are of even thickness.

Pour grape-seed or avocado oil in a 13" x 9" baking dish.

Lightly dredge the chicken through to coat it, then place chicken breasts side by side in the dish.

In a small bowl, whisk together salt, pepper, garlic powder, onion powder, and chili powder.

Sprinkle the seasoning mixture over both sides of the chicken and rub it in with your hands.

Place chicken breasts side by side, making sure there is no overlap.

Bake in a preheated oven for 15-20 minutes, until juices are clear, or a meat thermometer reads 160-170 degrees. *Note – depending on the size of your chicken breasts, it could take longer. Mine were pounded to less than an inch thick.

Cover with foil and allow to rest for 5-10 minutes while the juices settle before slicing.

Add a sweet potato or quinoa and a veggie

Yield 4-6 Servings

Coconut Chicken Tenders

Ingredients:

- 1 package of all-natural white meat chicken tenders
- 2 flax eggs (2 TBSP flax and 5 TBSP water, let sit for 5 mins or until thick)
- ¼ cup canned coconut milk
- 1 TBSP sriracha sauce
- 1 ½ cup unsweetened flaked coconut
- ¾ cup wheat gluten-free Panko bread crumbs
- 1 tsp sea salt
- ½ tsp fresh black pepper
- ¼ tsp cayenne (optional)
- sweet red chili sauce for dipping (optional)

Directions:

In a medium bowl whisk together the flax eggs, milk, and sriracha sauce. Set aside.

In a medium, shallow dish, combine the coconut, panko, salt, pepper, and cayenne. Dip the chicken strips in the egg mixture to coat, and then into the coconut mixture, coating completely. Transfer the chicken strips onto a plate and repeat the process with all the strips.

Turn the oven on to the lowest (or warm) setting, this is usually 160°F.

Line a large baking sheet with paper towels and set aside.

In a 10-inch frying pan fill the pan ⅓ inch deep with coconut oil.

Heat the oil over medium heat until it reaches a temperature of 375°F, or until small bubbles form when the back of a wooden spoon is placed in the oil.

In batches place the chicken in the pan, careful not to crowd the pan.

Fry 3-4 minutes on each side until golden brown. When the chicken is done, transfer to the paper towel-lined baking sheet and place in the oven to stay warm. Repeat with all the chicken.

Serve warm with dipping sauce, if desired.

Yield 4 -6 servings

Roasted Veggies and Sausage

Ingredients:

- 2 medium zucchinis, ends trimmed, sliced into half moons
- 2 medium yellow squash, ends trimmed, sliced into half moons
- 1 red bell pepper, diced into 3/4-inch squares
- ½ large red onion, diced into 3/4-inch squares
- 8 oz button mushrooms, sliced thick
- 1 (10½ oz) package grape or cherry tomatoes; halved
- 2 TBSP olive oil
- Salt and freshly ground black pepper
- 2 cloves garlic, minced
- 1 pkg all-natural chicken and apple sausage links
- 4 cups (4 oz) fresh spinach
- ⅔ cup homemade or store-bought pesto (recipe under dressings)
- Finely shredded Parmesan cheese or nutritional yeast, for serving

Directions:

Preheat oven to 425°F.

Place zucchini, squash, bell pepper, onion and mushrooms and sausage on a rimmed 18×13-inch baking sheet. Drizzle veggies with olive oil and season with salt and pepper then toss to evenly coat.

Roast in preheated oven 10 minutes, then remove, add tomatoes and garlic and toss.

Roast 10 minutes longer or until veggies are tender then remove add spinach and toss, roast 1 minute longer or until spinach has wilted.

Add in roasted veggies, chicken and pesto to a pan and season with salt and pepper to taste then toss to evenly coat and heat until warm and flavors combine about 5-7 minutes.

Serve warm, top each serving with Parmesan cheese or nutritional yeast.

Yield 4 -6 servings

Vinaigrettes, Dips and Seasonings

Apple Cider Vinaigrette

Ingredients:

- ¼ cup apple cider vinegar
- 5 TBSP extra virgin olive oil
- ½ TBSP coconut oil
- 1 tsp spicy brown mustard
- ½ tsp minced garlic
- 1 TBSP pure maple syrup (optional)

Directions:

Put all ingredients in a bottle or jar and shake

Can be used on meats, veggies, salad, etc.

Yield 8-10 servings

Chicken or Beef Spice Rub

Ingredients:

- ¼ cup paprika
- ¼ cup chili powder
- 1 TBSP onion powder
- 1 TBSP garlic powder
- 1-2 TBSP brown or coconut sugar (optional)
- Cayenne pepper to taste

Directions:

Mix all together and store in an airtight container for up to 6 months

Can be used as a dry rub on chicken or beef

Yield 14 servings

Red Wine Vinaigrette

Ingredients:

- ½ cup olive oil
- 1 cup red wine vinegar
- 1 small lemon juiced
- 1 tsp minced garlic
- 1 tsp dried oregano
- salt and pepper to taste

Directions:

Mix everything in a jar and shake

Store in an airtight container at room temp

Keeps about 2 weeks

Yield 14 servings

Easy Detox Pesto

Ingredients:

- 2-3 garlic cloves, minced
- 4-5 TBSP pine nuts, almonds or walnuts
- 1 cup packed fresh basil leaves
- ½ cup extra virgin olive oil
- 1 TBSP lemon zest
- 1 TBSP fresh lemon juice
- ½ tsp sea salt

Directions:

Use a food processor or blender. Chop garlic first. Add nuts and chop again. Add basil, chop or blend well.

Feed olive oil in while the machine is running.

Add sea salt, to taste for texture.

Yield: 8-10 servings

Clean Taco Seasoning

Ingredients:

- 1 TBSP chili powder
- 1 tsp ground cumin
- 1 tsp garlic powder
- 1 tsp paprika
- ½ tsp oregano
- ½ tsp onion powder
- ¼ tsp sea salt
- ¼ tsp black pepper
- ¼ tsp crushed red pepper flakes (optional)

Directions:

Whisk all ingredients together in a small bowl (or shake together in a jar) until combined.

Store in an airtight container for up to 6 months.

In general, I recommend using 2-3 TBSP of seasoning per pound of meat.

Homemade Almond Milk

Ingredients:

Unsweetened Almond Milk:
- o 1 cup raw almonds, soaked and drained
- o 3 cups filtered water
- o Pinch of sea salt

Sweetened Milk (Unsweetened Milk, Plus Below):
- o 1 tsp natural vanilla extract
- o 3-6 pitted dates (or 2-3 TBSP pure maple syrup or sweetener)
- o 1 TBSP melted virgin coconut oil (or raw almond butter, optional)

Chocolate Almond Milk (Sweetened Milk, Plus Below):
- o 2 TBSP raw cacao powder, plus more to taste

Cinnamon Milk (Sweetened Milk, Plus Below):
- o 1 tsp ground cinnamon, plus more to taste

Strawberry Milk (Sweetened Milk, Plus Below):
- o 3 cups fresh strawberries, plus more to taste

Directions:

To soak the almonds, place the nuts in a glass bowl and cover with filtered water. Add a pinch of sea salt and splash of fresh lemon juice or apple cider vinegar. Cover the container with a breathable kitchen towel and allow to soak at room temperature for 12 hours.

Drain and discard the soaking liquid (do not use this to make the milk). Rinse the almonds several times to remove the anti-nutrients and enzyme inhibitors.

Throw the rinsed almonds, water, and salt in your blender, and blast on high for 30 to 60 seconds, until the nuts are completely pulverized. Use whole milk to maximize nutrition. Or strain for a smoother, more commercial-style milk for use in recipes.

To strain, place a nut milk bag or knee-high piece of sheer nylon hosiery over the opening of a glass bowl. Pour the milk into the bag, twisting the bag closed, and gently squeezing it to pass the liquid through. Empty the almond pulp aside. Rinse your blender container, and pour the strained milk back in. Add the vanilla, sweetener, and any flavorings, and blast again, until smooth and creamy.

Homemade Guacamole

Ingredients:

- 4 ripe Haas avocados
- ¼ red onion chopped
- ¼ cup pomegranate seeds or dried cranberries
- ¼ cup cilantro leaves, chopped (no stems)
- ¼ tsp sea salt
- 1 TBSP lime juice, squeeze from 3 key limes
- Garnish with cilantro

Directions:

Using a knife or avocado tool, slice avocados in half. Reserve the pits for later.

Remove the peels and place the avocado in a bowl.

Mash the avocados until the consistency is smooth with just a few small lumps.

Add remaining ingredients to the bowl. Gently fold all ingredients together.

Garnish with a few cilantro leaves.

Enjoy with chopped veggies.

If your guacamole will not be enjoyed right away, add in an avocado pit or two, and squeeze a bit more lime juice on top. This will help the guacamole from turning brown.

Dessert

Yummy Fertility Brownies

Ingredients:

- 1 flax egg
- 15 oz can low sodium black beans, rinsed and drained
- ½ large, ripe avocado
- 1 TBSP vanilla extract
- ½ cup brown sugar

- ⅔ cup raw cacao
- ¼ tsp organic baking soda
- ½ tsp baking powder
- ⅓ cup vegan dark chocolate chips, plus 2 TBSP for sprinkling
- ½ tsp organic coconut oil

Directions:

Preheat oven to 350°F and grease an 8×8 baking dish

Place flax egg, black beans, avocado, vanilla, and brown sugar and mix in a food processor until smooth

Add raw cacao, baking soda and baking powder and process again until smooth. The batter should be thick. If the batter is way too thick and won't process, add in 1-2 TBSP of almond milk. The batter needs to be very thick to produce the fudgy brownies you want.

Fold in chocolate chips or sprinkle into the batter then transfer to prepared baking pan and use a spatula to spread evenly to sides. Sprinkle the top of the batter with 2 TBSP of remaining chocolate chips.

Bake for 22-30 minutes or until a knife in center comes out clean. We don't want these to dry out, but we also don't want them raw either.

The top of the batter should be completely set and no longer jiggle.

Cool pan completely on a wire rack then cut into 12 bars.

Top with almond slivers.

Yield: 12 servings

Fudgy Fudge

Ingredients:

- 1 cup organic coconut oil
- ¾ cup raw honey
- 1 cup all-natural raw cacao

Directions:

Melt coconut oil.

Put melted oil, honey and cocoa powder in a blender; blend on high.

Pour into wax paper lined pan (I use a 9x5 inch loaf pan and it's a perfect size).

Chill in fridge or freezer

Once firm, cut and serve.

Store in the fridge.

Variations:

Add vanilla, coffee beans, 2-3 drops peppermint extract, orange zest, nuts, " tsp. sea salt.... really, the options are endless!

Edible Cookie Dough

Ingredients:

- 1 cup almond flour
- ¼ cup coconut flour
- ¼ cup + 1 TBSP pure maple syrup
- 3 TBSP refined coconut oil melted
- 1 TBSP vanilla extract
- a couple of big pinches of sea salt
- ¼ cup dairy-free dark chocolate chips

Directions:

Stir together all ingredients, except chocolate chips, until very well combined. Stir in chocolate chips. Serve or chill.

Chocolate Fiber Balls

Ingredients:

- ¼ cup rolled oats
- 1 cup dried prunes
- 3 TBSP almond butter
- 1 TBSP raw honey
- 2 TBSP raw cacao
- 1 scoop your favorite chocolate protein powder (28g scoop)
- ¼ cup mini chocolate chips (optional)

Directions:

In the bowl of your food processor, blend oats into a flour-like texture. Add prunes, nut-free butter, honey, cacao powder, and protein powder, and process mixture until

Remove the blades from the food processor and fold in mini chocolate chips.

Begin rolling out the dough by hand, about a TBSP at a time and place bites into a container. Refrigerate for 30 minutes until set.

Decadent Almond Butter Brownies

Ingredients:

- 2 cage-free eggs
- 1 cup almond butter or nut butter of choice
- ⅓ cup raw honey
- ⅓ cup organic raw cacao powder
- 1 TBSP pure vanilla extract
- ½ tsp baking soda
- ⅓ cup dark chocolate chips (optional)

Directions:

Preheat oven to 325°F.

Line an 8×8-inch baking pan with parchment paper. Set aside.

In a large bowl place, the eggs, honey, almond butter, and vanilla extract.

Whisk to combine.

Stir in cacao powder and baking soda until combined.

Fold in dark chocolate chips if using.

Pour the batter into the prepared pan and smooth the top with a spatula.

Bake in preheated oven for 20-23 minutes or until a toothpick inserted in center comes out clean.

Cut into squares and serve.

Peanut Butter Mug Cake

Ingredients:

- ⅛ cup natural creamy peanut butter (only ground peanuts and salt)
- ⅛ cup all-natural almond butter
- 1 large egg
- 1 tsp of raw honey
- ¼ tsp baking soda

Directions:

In a medium mug or a large ramekin, mix the peanut butter with the egg until completely incorporated. Check the bottom closely to make sure there is no peanut butter residue remaining.

If the batter seems very thick, sticky and stubborn, add a TBSP of water and keep mixing until completely smooth. Mix in the stevia, then the baking soda. Mix well. Microwave the peanut butter mug cake for 30 seconds. Check it – if it looks very wet, add 10 more seconds. I usually stop at this point – the edges are puffed and done but the center is still gooey. That's how I like it!

Enjoy the cake as is or top it with a dollop of stevia-sweetened whipped cream for a truly rich experience.

Chocolate "Nice" Cream

Ingredients:

- 2 frozen bananas cut in chunks
- 1 TBSP all-natural peanut butter or almond butter
- 1 TBSP raw cacao powder

Directions:

Put all ingredients into a food processor and process until crumbles start to form. 1-2 mins

Scrape down the sides of the food processor.

Process another 3-4 mins until a creamy, soft serve like ice cream forms

Eat immediately or freeze for a harder consistency

Suggested toppings-
- 1 TBSP walnuts, almonds or cashews
- 1 TBSP unsweetened coconut
- 1 TBSP coconut cream
- 1 TBSP enjoy life vegan chocolate chips

Yield 2 servings

Berry "Nice" Cream

Ingredients:

- 2-3 frozen bananas
- ½ cup frozen cherries
- pinch of sea salt
- ⅛ tsp pure vanilla extract
- Handful of cherries

Directions:

Start with bananas that are turning brown. Peel and cut into large pieces, then freeze in an airtight bag or container. (You can freeze a whole bunch at once so they're ready whenever you want to make banana ice cream.) To make the ice cream, throw frozen bananas, frozen cherries, and ⅛ tsp vanilla into a blender or food processor—adding a pinch of salt and 2-4 TBSP milk of choice for smoother blending if desired—and blend until you achieve a soft serve texture.

You can serve immediately or transfer to a container and freeze an additional 30 minutes, then scoop out with an ice cream scoop.

Top with cherries or any other toppings you desire

Yield 2 servings

CC Almond Butter Energy Balls

Ingredients:

- 1 cup gluten-free old-fashioned oats
- ⅔ cup unsweetened toasted coconut flakes
- ½ cup all-natural almond butter
- ½ cup ground flax seeds
- ¼ cup dark chocolate chips (optional)
- ⅓ cup coconut oil
- 1 tsp chia seeds
- 1 tsp pure vanilla extract

Directions:

Stir all ingredients together in a medium bowl until thoroughly mixed.

Cover and let chill in the refrigerator for half an hour.

Once chilled, roll into balls of whatever size you would like. (Mine were about 1" in diameter.)

Roll in coconut flakes

Store in an airtight container and keep refrigerated for up to 1 week.

Yield 12 servings

Healthy Peanut Butter Cup

Ingredients:

For the peanut butter bottoms:
- o   1 cup organic peanut butter
- o   ¼ cup organic maple syrup
- o   ¼ cup organic coconut oil (melted/liquid)

For the chocolate topping:
- o   ¼ cup organic raw cacao powder
- o   ⅛ – ¼ cup organic maple syrup
- o   ¼ cup organic coconut oil (melted/liquid)

Directions:

Add all the ingredients for the peanut butter bottoms to a medium-sized bowl and stir until well combined, creamy and smooth.

Drop a spoonful at a time into standard size muffin cups until they are approximately ½ – ⅔ full.

Put them in the freezer for at least 15 minutes, or until slightly hardened.

Prepare the chocolate topping:

Add all the ingredients for the chocolate topping to a small size bowl and stir until well combined, creamy and smooth.

Assembly:

Remove the peanut butter cups from the freezer and drop 1-2 spoonful's of the chocolate topping on top of each peanut butter cup, making sure you have a solid thin layer.

Return the peanut butter cups back into the freezer for about 30-60 minutes, or until they are hardened.

Keep in the freezer until ready to serve because they will get soft and lose their shape if left out at room temperature.

Yield 8 servings

Please use these recipes as you are doing the fertility reset. These recipes are written so that they are easy to prepare, aid in reset and are delicious. You can also make your own based on the approved foods list found in Chapter 2. Get creative and enjoy some uncommon foods.

Have fun!

You deserve it.

coachkela's Recipe Book

28-Day Reset

Let's dig in

Get ready to jump start your weight loss and healthy life.

Welcome to your **recipe guide**. This will have all the info in it to make the recipes suggested for your reset. These recipes are written based on the balanced nutrition that Kela teaches, and the ingredients included in each one has the **correct number of macros** to efficiently **fuel your body and jump start your metabolism**, so you start to heal your body from the inside out, eliminate toxic build up so your energy goes up and the weight starts to fall off. If there are ingredients that you just can't stand or won't eat, you can make substitutions based on the approved foods however, make sure the macros (protein, fat, carbs and fiber) are still the same and are balanced. Coach Kela can help you with this. **The recipes on the first few pages will follow Coach Kela's guidelines for the first week** and the recipes that follow are substitutions that you can make.

✓ Get rid of any "toxic temptations" in your home & work environment.

✓ Plan out time for prep, cooking and recording notes in your journal.

28 game changing days that will get you to the finish line!

Starting Line-up

You will eat from these recipes (breakfast, lunch, and dinner) for Week 1 as directed in the 28-Day Reset Manual.

Week 2 You can continue with these recipes as well as adding in some of the re-introduction foods or you can pick substitution recipes from the additional recipes section.

Breakfast

Rise and Shine! / Breakfast

Upon rising, drink an 8oz glass of warm lemon water. Follow with flaxseed cocktail. During the next 15 minutes breathe, stretch, walk outside, skin brush and bathe, ending with a cool rinse. Eat breakfast and Detox tea (after you eat)

The Flax Seed Cocktail

You are to drink the flax seed cocktail on an empty stomach each and every morning and night to help with elimination.

Add flax seeds to the 8oz of water and stir. Drink quickly. Do not let it sit too long or it will coagulate! Follow with a second glass of water.

Warm Lemon Water

Drink warm lemon water upon waking up and again before bedtime. It can also be used to shake off cravings mid-day if needed. This helps with elimination and to clean the intestines.

- o *1 8 oz cup filtered water*
- o *½ to 1 organic lemon*

Heat water to desired temperature = warm. Squeeze ½ to 1 lemon in it and drink...enjoy!

Breakfast

(Unless noted: makes 1 Serving)

The Touch Down Shake

o   ½ cup frozen spinach
o   1 cup frozen cherries
o   ¼ frozen avocado
o   1 TBSP almond butter
o   2 tsp maca root powder 1 tsp spirulina
o   2 scoops pea or rice protein powder
o   2-3 ice cubes
o   1 cup (approx.) unsweetened almond milk

Layer ingredients from top to bottom of the list (almond milk goes in last)! Blend all ingredients in a Nutra ninja or strong blender. Drink in a pretty glass with a straw...yummmmmm!

Cream of Rice Cereal

o   ¼ cup rice cereal 1¼ cup water
o   ½ cup blueberries
o   ¼ cup soaked pumpkin seeds pinch of ginger powder
o   A pinch of cinnamon
o   ¼ cup rice milk tiny pinch of stevia

Bring the water to a boil in a small pot. Add the salt and rice cereal mixing well. Reduce the heat and simmer until cereal becomes thicker, stirring frequently. When at desired thick- ness, remove from heat and place in a bowl. Stir in blueberries, rice milk, nuts, spices, and stevia. Eat warm

The Fifty-Yard Line Shake

o   2 cups frozen mangos
o   2 TBSP dried, (shredded) unsweetened coconut
o   2 scoops pea or rice protein powder
o   1 tsp of lime juice
o   1-2 ice cubes
o   1 cup unsweetened coconut water or milk

Blend all ingredients in a Nutra ninja or strong blender – layer ingredients putting in coconut water or milk last.

Make The Goal / Healthy Rice Bread

o   1-2 pieces of rice bread
o   1 TBSP nut butter
o   ½ avocado

Toast bread until desired doneness, spread ½ tbsp of nut butter on each piece, top with avocado, sprinkle with a small dash of black pepper or cinnamon.

Mid-Morning

Snack, if needed, fruit, veggies, small handful of nuts. Breathe. Drink water. You got this!

Lunch

Enjoy your lunch, have some detox tea. If the weather permits, sun gaze (stand out- side, gaze at the sun with your eyes closed, feel the warm sunlight on the backs of your eyelids.) or a 5 min meditation

Yummy Olive Oil Dressing

- o 1 clove of garlic crushed
- o ½ cup virgin cold pressed olive oil
- o ¼ apple cider vinegar
- o ¼ tsp Celtic or himalayan sea salt
- o ¼ tsp black pepper
- o ½ tsp basil, oregano, and thyme

Makes a huge bottle. This can be kept in the fridge for up to 3 weeks. Only use 1-2 TBSP per serving.

Avocado and Basil Dressing

- o 2 cups fresh basil
- o ½ lemon, juiced
- o 1 tsp celtic salt
- o ¾ cup olive oil
- o ½ avocado
- o 2 TBSP apple cider vinegar

Put all ingredients into a blender and blend until smooth. Makes a pretty big bottle. This can be kept in the fridge for up to 3 weeks. Only use 1-2 TBSP per serving.

Gimme Green Salad
(3 to 4 Servings)

- o 1 bunch dino kale
- o 1 bunch purple cabbage shredded coarsely
- o 2 scallions
- o 1 cup toasted pumpkin seeds
- o ½ avocado
- o Optional: fresh herbs to taste-try mint or cilantro

Dressing:
- o 2 cloves garlic (pressed or minced)
- o ¼ cup rice vinegar
- o ½ cup olive oil
- o 2 TBSP toasted sesame oil

Wash the greens. Chop kale leaves by rolling them into a tube and slicing very thinly, creating narrow strips. Combine all salad ingredients in a large bowl. Blend the dressing ingredients, pour over salad and mingle well. Set aside for 20 minutes or for best results overnight. The dressing will last for a few days in the refrigerator so make extra
(Add the avocado just before serving or it will get mushy. If you love it, double it! This recipe gets better each day.)

Rainbow Salad *(3 to 4 Servings)*

- o 1 carrot shredded
- o 1 cup purple cabbage shredded
- o 1 small ripe avocado cut into small chunks
- o 1 zucchini or yellow squash thinly sliced
- o 1-2 celery stalks diced
- o ½ cup jicama, diced (optional)
- o ½ cup sunflower seeds

Place all ingredients into a salad bowl and toss lightly. Dress with 1-2 TBSP of dressings from the dressing recipes

Basic Stir-Fry *(4 To 6 Servings)*

- o ¼ cup veggie broth
- o 1 lb chicken or fish (omit if doing vegetarian)
- o 2 cups mushrooms (try shiitake rimini, oyster or chicken of the woods)
- o 2 carrots cut in matchsticks 1 tsp fresh grated ginger 2-3 cups chopped kale
- o ¼ tsp cayenne pepper (optional)
- o Celtic sea salt to taste

Heat broth in a non-stick skillet over medium-high heat. Add (meat), mushrooms, carrots and ginger. Cook for 5 minutes. Add remaining ingredients, cook until tender. Kale should still be bright green, do not overcook.
Serving size is 1-2 cups. Make sure to listen to your hunger and follow the suggested serving sizes on the sample menu

Late Afternoon

Snack, if needed, fruit, veggies, small handful of nuts. Breathe. Drink water. Belly massage. Connect with your support tools or people.

Lunch

Dinner

Drink warm lemon water 20 min before dinner, then have dinner with detox tea. Do any support activities ex: breathe, gentle exercise, walk, skin brush and bathe (if you didn't do it in the morning). The body goes into deep detox mode at night. Complete your last meal by 7 pm and do not consume any other food until the next morning. Your body needs about 12 hours to fully clean house!

Gentle Lentil Soup (4 To 6 Servings)

- o 1 cup dried lentils
- o 6 cups filtered water
- o 1 strip wakame seaweed cut into ½ inch pieces
- o 1 onion diced
- o 2 cloves garlic minced
- o 1 carrot sliced diagonally
- o 1 parsnip sliced diagonally
- o 1 cup kale or spinach loosely chopped
- o 3 TBSP brown rice or garbanzo miso

Layer lentils, wakame, onion, garlic, carrot and parsnip in a pot. Pour in the water, bring to a boil and simmer for 45 minutes. Add greens and simmer for another 5 minutes. Dissolve miso into soup just before serving.

Thai Squash Stew (4 To 6 Servings)

- o 2 TBSP coconut oil
- o 3 garlic cloves finely chopped
- o 1 medium leek (white parts only)
- o 1 TBSP finely chopped ginger
- o 1 TBSP curry powder
- o 1 15 oz. can unsweetened coconut milk
- o 1-2 lbs butternut squash peeled & cubed
- o salt to taste
- o juice of 1 lime

Cut the leeks into half-moons and wash well in water. Heat the oil in a wide soup pot. Add the leeks and cook over medium-high heat, stirring frequently, until partially softened, about 3 minutes. Add the garlic and ginger, cook 1 minute more, then add the curry. Reduce the heat to medium, and add 3 cups water, the coconut milk, squash, and 1 tsp. salt. Bring to a boil. Then lower the heat and simmer, covered, for 15 minutes or until the squash melts in your mouth. Add the lime juice and salt if needed

Want more options?

Read on for more inspiration and tasty meals.

Any of the following recipes in the guide can be swapped out for the suggested meal planning for the 28-Day reset. These recipes are written based on the balanced nutrition plan and you can feel confident to mix and match meals for variety.

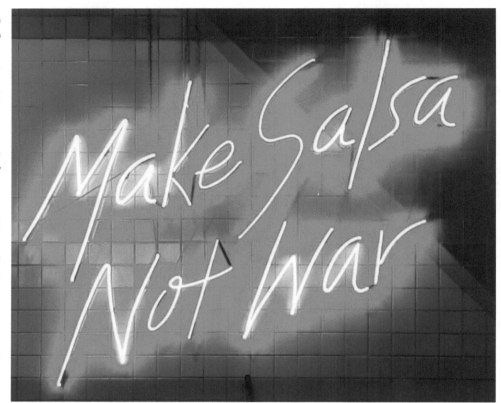

Fish or Chicken Tacos (2 Servings)

- o 8-12 oz firm white fish (halibut or cod)
- o ½ cup coconut milk
- o ¾ cup shredded coconut
- o 1 TBSP curry powder
- o 1 tsp sea salt
- o 4 large romaine lettuce leaves (as shells)

Mango Salsa:
- o 1 ripe mango peeled & diced
- o ¼ inch add cilantro (to taste)
- o 2 tsp grated ginger root (peeled)
- o fresh squeezed juice
- o zest of 1 lime

Skin the fish and cut into ½ inch thick slices. Dunk each piece in the coconut milk, then into the curry-coconut mixture. Coat on all sides. Cook each fish in coconut oil over medium heat until both sides are brown. Make the mango salsa by combining all ingredients. Serving size is 2 tacos and ¼ cup of mango salsa.

Additional Recipes

Super Veggie Soup (6 To 8 Servings)

- o 6 to 8 cups veggie stock
- o 2 onions
- o 2 green onions
- o 3 celery stalks
- o 3 carrots
- o 3 zucchini
- o 4 garlic cloves pressed
- o 3 kale leaves
- o 3 cups broccoli florets
- o 1 bulb fennel
- o ½ bunch Italian parsley
- o ½ bunch cilantro
- o 1 TBSP olive oil

Cut veggies in small pieces, except for kale and broccoli / coarsely chop. In a large pot sauté onion, green onions, celery, carrots, fennel, zucchini and garlic in oil for 5 min. Add broth and bring to a boil, simmer, covered for another 5 minutes.

Stir in broccoli for 3 minutes. Add kale, parsley and cilantro. Cover and remove pot from heat for 2 minutes. Serve.

Serving size is 1 cup.

Simple Veggie Broth (6 To 8 Servings)

- o 2 quarts filtered water
- o 1 large onion cut into 1-inch pieces
- o 2 stalks celery cut into 1-inch pieces
- o 2 carrots peeled and cut into 1-inch pieces
- o 8 cloves garlic crushed
- o 8 sprigs fresh parsley
- o 2 bay leaves
- o 1 large piece of kombu seaweed (optional but does add great flavor!)

Place all ingredients in a large stockpot and bring to a boil. Lower heat and simmer for 1 hour. Strain. Eat or discard the vegetables. Refrigerate and use within 3 days or freeze. Serving size is 1 cup

Hint of Mint Quinoa (4 To 6 Servings)

- o 2 cups quinoa
- o 3½ cups water
- o 1 bag peppermint tea
- o 1 TBSP olive oil
- o fresh mint
- o fresh basil
- o fresh cilantro

Place quinoa, water, and peppermint tea bag in a saucepan. Bring to a boil. Cover and simmer for 15-20 minutes. When done, add olive oil, fluff, and serve. Garnish with chopped fresh herbs. Serving size 1 cup.

Red Quinoa with Pumpkin Seeds and Kale (4 To 6 Servings)

- o 1 cup red quinoa (pre-soaked or thoroughly rinsed)
- o ¼ raw pumpkin seeds
- o 1-2 TBSP sesame oil
- o 1 bunch red Russian kale, rinsed and chopped

Bring quinoa, salt and water to a boil. Cover and simmer on medium-low for 15 minutes. Heat sesame oil in a skillet on medium heat. Add pumpkin seeds and lower heat, stirring and toasting for 1 minute. Add kale. Stir fry for 2-3 minutes until kale is tender but still bright green. Toss with quinoa. Serving size 1 cup.

Quinoa with Caramelized Onions

- o 1 cup quinoa (pre-soaked or thoroughly rinsed)
- o 2 cups water
- o 1 TBSP olive oil
- o 1 onion cut into thick crescents
- o 1 zucchini cut into circles
- o pinch of Salt

Bring quinoa, salt and water to a boil. Cover and simmer on medium-low for 15 minutes. Meanwhile, heat olive oil in a skillet. Add onion and cook for 3 minutes until the onion starts to caramelize. Add zucchini and a splash of water. Cover and cook until tender.
The zucchini should be slightly translucent but still bright green. Toss veggies and feta with quinoa and eat!

Baked Carrot Oven Fries (4 Servings)

- o one bunch of organic carrots unpeeled washed & trimmed
- o 3 TBSP extra virgin olive oil
- o sea salt

Chop the green leafy tops off the carrots. Line a baking sheet with foil. Arrange carrots in a single layer on the baking sheet, toss with olive oil and sprinkle generously with salt. Bake for 25-30 minutes or until carrots are golden brown where they touch the pan.

Baked Salmon with Pesto, Lemon and Dill
(2 Servings)

- o 2 wild salmon fillets (any desired amount)
- o ¼ cup olive oil
- o ½ lemon 1 tsp dill

Pesto:
- o 2-3 cloves garlic chopped fine
- o 4-5 TBSP pine nuts, almonds or walnuts
- o 1 cup packed fresh basil leaves
- o ½ cup olive oil
- o ½ tsp Celtic salt

Salmon: Rinse salmon and pat dry with a paper towel. Rub olive oil onto the inside of a baking dish, and place salmon inside. Rub any remaining olive oil onto the salmon. Squeeze lemon onto salmon and sprinkle with dill. Bake until just done, do not overcook. Remove from oven and top with pesto. (recipe below). Serving size 1 filet with 1-2 TBSP of pesto.

Pesto: Use a food processor or blender. Chop garlic first. Add nuts and chop again. Add basil, chop or blend well. Feed olive oil in while machine is running. Add sea salt, taste for texture, adjust if needed.
Makes a huge jar. Will keep on the counter for 2 weeks.
Serving size 1-2 TBSP.

Mixed Greens Salad
(3 To 4 Servings)

- o 1 bunch collard greens
- o 1 bunch kale
- o 1 cup arugula
- o 1 red cabbage chopped
- o 1 carrot grated
- o 1 beet grated
- o 1 watermelon radish peeled and sliced
- o ½ cup pumpkin seeds
- o ½ cup butter beans (best from a jar, not canned.)
- o nutritional yeast (optional)

Tear the greens or chop into thin ribbons. Add chopped cabbage, carrot, beet and daikon. Sprinkle pumpkin seeds and beans. Top with one of the dressings (1 TBSP) and nutritional yeast
Serving size is 1-2 cups.
If made generously, this salad can be enough for a meal. The seeds and beans add protein and essential fatty acids, making it satisfying and substantial.
Yummmm!

The Green Dragon (1 To 2 Servings)

- o 1½ cups warm water
- o 2 TBSP south river miso (preferably adzuki bean or chick pea)
- o 2 cups spinach
- o 1-2 collard or kale leaves
- o ¼ avocado
- o ¼ lemon cut off yellow but leave white pith
- o 1 tsp dried oregano
- o ½ cup fresh basil
- o 1 tsp chipotle powder

Add all ingredients to a blender. Blend well and enjoy! Makes 1 -2 servings. Serving size is 1 cup.

Super Green Soup (2 Servings)

- o 1 cup cucumber peeled and diced
- o 2 packed cups fresh spinach leaves
- o ¼ cup arugula
- o 1 cup sprouts (any sprouts will do)
- o 1 avocado peeled, pitted and diced
- o A pinch of salt
- o 1 tsp of fresh lemon juice
- o ¼ cup TBSP of fresh cilantro

Add all ingredients to a blender. Mix 10 seconds until blended, but not completely smooth. Ladle into a bowl or mug and serve. Serving size 1 cup. Note: If you'd like to add some variety experiment with changing up the flavor by adding different herbs such as dill, basil or sorrel!

Rejuvenator

- 1 bunch of kale
- 4 ribs of celery
- 1 cucumber
- 1 burdock root
- 1 lemon
- 1-2 apples peeled

Rinse all ingredients. Shave apple skin. Throw everything in a juicer!
Drink immediately.

Juiced Boosts

Enlightener

- 2 handfuls of greens (lettuce, kale) meat from 2 fresh young coconuts
- 2 small avocados

Toss into a blender and pulse for 4 seconds. Then blend.

High Performer

- 1 glass of coconut water
- 1 tsp of spirulina

Spirulina is the highest protein food on the planet. Coconut water (packaged is fine — preferably in glass) is the highest source of electrolytes. This is a great athletic booster

Cilantro Power Soup

- 2 small bunches cilantro
- 1 clove garlic
- juice of ½ lemon
- 1 cup walnuts or pumpkin seeds
- 2 TSBP garbanzo miso
- 1 TSBP flax oil or half an avocado
- water to blend (about 2-3 cups)

Put all ingredients in a blender. Add 2 cups of water, blend, adding water as you go to blend smoothly. Avocado will create a creamier texture. Garnish and eat immediately. Optional: add scallions, chopped avocado as garnish.

Creamy Miso (1 To 2 Servings)

- 1 cup water
- 1 cup cucumber and/or cilantro
- ½ avocado
- 1 ½ tsp garbanzo or adzuki miso paste
- 1 tsp fresh ginger
- 1 tsp chopped scallions

Toss into a blender and pulse for 4 seconds. Should have chunky consistency. You can experiment by adding ¼ cup of daikon radish or ½ cup bok choy. Serving size is 1 cup.

Treat!

Baked Apple (3 Servings)

- 3 apples, cored
- 2 tsp cinnamon
- 1 tsp vanilla

Preheat to 350°F. Blend a few tbsp of water with the vanilla. Drizzle into and over the apple in a baking dish add cinnamon. Bake for 20 minutes.
Optional; cut a small mochi and place it in the core of the apple about last 6 mins of baking.

Your Fertility
Meal Plan

Recipe Guide

Breakfast

Mint Chocolate Chip Smoothie

Veggie and Mushroom Frittata

Fertility Boost Juice

Apple Pie Date Sweet Oatmeal

Lunch

Beef and Broccoli Stir-Fry

Shrimp and Veggies with Fried Rice

Fertility Salad

Salmon Sushi Bowl

Dinner

Forbidden Rice with Chicken and Spring Veggies

Italian Spiced Roasted Chicken with Sweet Potatoes

White Bean Soup with Kale, Rosemary and Garlic

Fertility Boost (Meat) Balls

Breakfast

Mint Chocolate Chip Smoothie

Ingredients:

- 1 frozen organic banana
- 1 TBSP almond butter
- 3-5 oz canned coconut milk
- 1-2 TBSP raw cacao
- 1 tsp vanilla or peppermint extract
- ½ tsp maca root powder
- ½ tsp spirulina powder
- bee pollen to taste

Directions:

Blend until creamy in a Vitamix or high-speed blender.

Served in a pretty glass with a straw.

Top with a sprinkle of dark chocolate chips.

Veggie and Mushroom Frittata

Ingredients:

- 1 dozen free range eggs
- 2 cups organic white mushrooms
- 1 bunch asparagus
- ¼ cup canned coconut milk
- ¼ cup pecorino cheese
- 1 TBSP olive oil
- ½ tsp salt
- pepper to taste

Salad-

- 5 cups mixed baby spinach
- ½ cup buttermilk
- ⅓ cup apple cider vinegar
- ¼ cup extra virgin olive oil
- 1 TBSP chopped dill
- 1 tsp dried mustard
- ¼ tsp black pepper
- salt to taste

Directions:

Preheat oven to 350°F.

Whisk eggs, coconut milk, and salt together in a large bowl

Chop mushrooms, and sauté gently over medium heat with 1 TBSP olive oil

When mushrooms begin to soften and release moisture, add the asparagus, chopped into 1" pieces, sauté until aromatic and bright green.

Fold vegetables into the egg mix and then pour into a hot, greased cast iron and place in the oven until it begins to set in the middle.

When it is almost solid, pull the frittata out and cover with grated pecorino cheese and replace under the broiler for 30 seconds - 2 minutes (watch closely so it doesn't burn)

Whisk together dressing ingredients except for olive oil, once emulsified slowly pour olive oil in until combine. Drizzle dressing over mixed greens and serve with a slice of frittata.

Fertility Boost Juice

Ingredients:

- 6 carrots
- 3 cups of cilantro
- 2 garlic cloves
- 2 cups broccoli florets
- ½ of an apple

Directions:

Use a juicer to extract liquid, chill and enjoy.

Apple Pie Date Sweet Oatmeal

Ingredients:

- 2 tart or sweet apples (peeled, cored and evenly sliced)
- 1 TBSP raw honey/maple syrup (optional)
- ¼ tsp ground cinnamon
- 1 tsp lemon juice
- 1 cup gluten-free old-fashioned rolled oats
- 1 cup water
- 1 cup dairy-free milk (I used unsweetened almond or canned coconut milk)
- 1 pinch sea salt
- 4 whole dates (finely chopped)
- peaches (optional topping)

Directions:

Preheat oven to 350°F (176°C).

Line a baking sheet with parchment paper and toss apples with lemon juice, cinnamon and honey. Bake for 5 minutes then roll over parchment paper and tuck it in so they're in a "pocket" to trap in moisture. Cook for 10-15 minutes more (20 minutes total) until soft. Set aside.

In a small saucepan over high heat, add oats, pinch salt, water and almond milk and stir. When it comes to a boil, reduce to low-medium heat and cook until thick and creamy. Add the chopped dates a few minutes after you reduce the heat so they can soften and sweeten the oats.

Once thick, remove from the stovetop. Add a little almond milk if it's too thick for your liking.

Arrange ⅓ cup of baked apples in the bottom of a serving bowl and top with oats. Other toppings may include, nuts, nut butter, flaxseed, honey, maple syrup, or cinnamon. I prefer mine with a few toasted pecans and flaxseed.

Lunch

Beef and Broccoli Stir-Fry

Ingredients:

- 1 ¼ lbs flank steak thinly sliced
- 1 TBSP + 1 tsp coconut oil divided use
- 2 cups broccoli florets
- 1-2 sweet potatoes - chopped
- 1 cup spinach chopped
- 2 tsp minced fresh ginger
- 1 tsp minced garlic

- ¼ cup oyster sauce
- ¼ cup beef broth or water
- 1 tsp brown sugar
- 2 tsp toasted sesame oil
- 1 tsp soy sauce
- 1 tsp cornstarch
- salt and pepper to taste

Directions:

Bake broccoli and sweet potatoes in the oven on 400°F for 20 minutes

Sauté' ginger and garlic for a few minutes in a pan with some coconut oil.

Turn heat to high and add 1 TBSP of oil.

Season the steak pieces with salt and pepper and add them to the pan in a single layer. Cook for 3-4 minutes on each side until browned and cooked through.

Add the broccoli mixture back to the pan and cook for 2 more minutes or until warmed through.

In a bowl whisk together the oyster sauce, beef broth, brown sugar, sesame oil and soy sauce. In a small bowl mix the cornstarch with a TBSP of cold water.

Pour the oyster sauce mixture over the beef and vegetables; cook for 30 seconds. Add the cornstarch and bring to a boil; cook for 1 more minute or until the sauce has just started to thicken. Stir in spinach

Serve immediately, with brown rice or quinoa if desired.

Easy Baked Shrimp and Quinoa

Ingredients:

- 2 tsp sesame oil
- 2 tsp coconut oil
- 1 lb medium-large fresh shrimp, cleaned (approximately 15-20 count shrimp)
- 1 cup frozen peas and diced carrots blend (I don't thaw and use straight from the freezer)
- ½ cup corn (I use frozen straight from the freezer)
- 2 to 3 garlic cloves, finely minced or pressed
- ½ tsp ground ginger
- 3 large eggs, lightly beaten
- 4 cups cooked quinoa
- 2 to 3 green onions, trimmed and sliced into thin rounds
- 3 to 4 TBSP low-sodium soy sauce
- ½ tsp salt, or to taste
- ½ tsp freshly ground black pepper, or to taste

Directions:

To a large non-stick skillet or wok, add the oils and shrimp, cook over medium-high heat for about 3 minutes, flipping halfway through. Cooking time will vary based on the size of shrimp, don't overcook. Remove shrimp with a slotted spoon (allow oils and cooking juices to remain in the skillet) and place shrimp on a plate; set aside.

Add the peas, carrots, corn, and cook for about 2 minutes, or until vegetables begin to soften, stir intermittently.

Add the garlic, ginger, and cook for 1 minute, stir intermittently.

Push vegetables to one side of the skillet, add the eggs to the other side, and cook to scramble, stirring as necessary.

Add the shrimp, quinoa, green onions, evenly drizzle with soy sauce, evenly season with salt and pepper, and stir to combine. Cook for about 2 minutes, or until shrimp is reheated through. The recipe is best warm and fresh but will keep airtight in the fridge for up to 5 days or in the freezer for up to 4 months.

Fertility Salad

Ingredients:

- 2 cups rinsed and chopped Organic Romaine Lettuce (can sub butterhead, green-leaf or red-leaf lettuce)
- 1 cup chopped or sliced roasted chicken (can sub other proteins, black beans, fried eggs, turkey muffins)
- 1 whole small/medium avocado, sliced or diced
- 1 sheet sliced organic Nori or other seaweed
- 1 TBSP Goji berries
- 1 TBSP dried cranberries
- 10 organic olives
- 1 TBSP dried coconut
- 1 TBSP flaxseeds
- 1 TBSP chia seeds
- 1 TBSP walnuts
- Optional - Sprinkling of seeds based on where you are in your cycle- Pumpkin for pre-ovulatory, sesame or sunflower for luteal phase.

Dressing:

- 1 TBSP Organic Extra Virgin Olive Oil
- 1 TBSP Organic Apple Cider Vinegar
- 1 TBSP pure maple syrup
- 1 tsp ground mustard
- Sprinkle fresh ground pepper and sea salt

Directions:

Dressing –

Mix and shake.

Salad –

Mix everything in a large bowl and top with 1-2 TBSP of dressing.

Salmon Sushi Bowl

Ingredients:

- 1 ½ lbs wild-caught salmon
- 1 Avocado, sliced
- 1 cucumber, peeled and sliced
- 3 green onion, sliced
- 4 sheets nori, cut into strips
- sesame seeds for garnish (optional)
- Sushi Rice (see recipe below)
- Sriracha Aioli (see recipe below)
- Soy Ginger Dressing (see recipe below)
- For the Sushi Rice
- 2 cups jasmine rice or quinoa
- 3 Cups Water
- 2 TBSP rice vinegar
- 1 TBSP brown sugar
- ½ TBSP salt

For Soy Ginger Dressing –
- ½ cup low sodium soy sauce
- ¼ cup rice vinegar
- 2 tsp brown sugar
- 1 tsp sesame oil
- 1-2 TBSP fresh grated ginger root
- 3 garlic cloves, minced

For the Sriracha Aioli –
- ½ cup high-quality mayonnaise or veganaise
- 1-2 TBSP sriracha (to the desired spiciness)

Directions:

Bake salmon @ 425°F for 20-30 minutes until it is the desired doneness.

Cook quinoa or rice according to package directions.

In a small bowl, mix the rice vinegar, sugar and salt. Heat in the microwave for about 30 seconds, then stir until sugar and salt are dissolved. Pour vinegar mixture over the rice and stir until combined.

Prepare the sriracha aioli by stirring together the mayonnaise and sriracha, set aside.

Prepare the soy ginger dressing by stirring together the soy sauce, rice vinegar, sugar, sesame oil, ginger and garlic. Whisk until sugar is dissolved. Set aside.

To assemble Salmon Sushi Bowls, add sushi rice to the bowl. Top with a portion of salmon*, avocado, cucumber slices, green onion slices, and a few pieces of nori. Drizzle with sriracha aioli and soy ginger dressing. Garnish with sesame seeds if desired.

Dinner

Forbidden Rice with Minty Spring Vegetables

Ingredients:

- 1 cup forbidden rice
- 1 tsp salt
- 1 bunch asparagus, chopped in ½ inch pieces
- ¾ cup chickpeas
- ⅓ cup walnuts
- 1 TBSP mint
- ½ lemon, juiced
- ¼ cup olive oil
- salt and pepper to taste

Directions:

Pre-heat oven to 350°F.

Pour rice into a heavy bottomed pot and toast on medium heat for 3-5 minutes.

Cover rice with 2 cups filtered water, bring to a boil, reduce to a simmer and cover for 25 minutes. Remove from heat and set aside.

Roast asparagus in the oven on 400°F for 20 minutes. Mix with a little olive oil and brown sugar.

Heat chickpeas on the stove until warm.

Place walnuts on parchment paper and toast in oven until fragrant, 5-10 minutes.

In a small bowl, whisk together the mint, olive oil, and lemon juice incorporate olive oil slowly to create an emulsification. Salt and pepper to taste.

In a large bowl combine rice, vegetables, and dressing. Toss until well mixed and sprinkle with toasted walnuts.

Enjoy.

Italian Spiced Roasted Chicken

Ingredients:

- ½ pound roasted chicken breast, shredded
- 1 large head of cauliflower
- Italian spice blend
- 4 TBSP olive oil
- 1 TBSP turmeric
- ½ tsp cumin
- ½ tsp dry ginger
- ¼ tsp coriander
- ¼ tsp cardamom

- Cashew sauce
- 1 cup cashews
- ½ bunch cilantro
- ¼ cup nutritional yeast
- ¼ cup filtered water
- 2 garlic cloves
- 2 TBSP Dijon mustard
- 1 TBSP white wine vinegar
- salt and pepper to taste

Directions:

Preheat oven to 350°F.

Cut cauliflower in vertical slices and then into smaller, bite-sized pieces.

Mix Indian spice blend with olive oil and salt and smother cauliflower slices and bake for 30-40 minutes or until golden and tender.

In a blender, blend all of the cashew cheese ingredients until smooth and desired texture is reached.

Toss roasted chicken, warm cauliflower pieces and cover with creamy cashew sauce.

Source: Bauman college, Natural Chef Recipe Book.

White Bean Soup with Kale, Rosemary and Garlic

Ingredients:

- 1 medium yellow onion, small dice
- 1 medium carrot, small dice
- 1 celery rib, small dice
- 2 cloves garlic, minced
- chili flakes or aleppo pepper, to taste
- 1 sprig fresh rosemary, minced
- 4 cups dry or canned navy beans or white beans
- 4 cups vegetable stock
- sea salt & ground black pepper, to taste
- 2 TBSP fresh lemon juice
- 3 cups packed chopped organic kale (roughly 1 small bunch)
- big handful finely chopped flat-leaf parsley

Directions:

Add all the ingredients through to the vegetable stock to your crockpot and cook on low for 8 hours. The last 30 minutes of cooking add lemon juice and kale cook until kale is wilted and bright green. Top with parsley and avocado.

Fertility Boost (Meat) Balls

Ingredients:

- 2 lbs of organic ground beef or turkey
- 1 cup gluten-free bread crumbs
- 1 cup grated parmesan cheese
- ¼ cup fresh parsley or ⅛ cup dried
- ½ large organic diced onion
- 2 large farm fresh eggs
- 2 tsp dry oregano
- 2 tsp dry basil
- ½ tsp pepper
- salt to taste
- 1 TBSP coconut oil

Directions:

Combine all ingredients except oil in a bowl and mix well with hands.

Form one, 1½ inch meatballs (I use an ice cream scoop for size).

Preheat oven to 400 and place meatballs on a cookie sheet lined with foil. Drizzle coconut oil over the top.

Bake for 20-22 minutes. Watch for browning and pull when light brown.

Remove and let rest on paper towel.

Serve over pasta, on a meatball sub or by themselves.

The Final Puzzle Piece

Congratulations! You have finished this book and hopefully the online program. You should be pregnant or well on your way. I am so proud and excited for you and can't wait to see all the healthy babies we have created.

Please make sure you join my Facebook community,

The Hormone Puzzle - decoding hormones and fighting infertility naturally

In this group are women just like you who struggled or are struggling with infertility. This group is for support, encouragement, motivation as well as a place to share wins, big or small and talk through challenges. I am in the group weekly to answer questions and provide tips and tricks on how to get pregnant quicker and with ease, naturally.

If you are pregnant, let's celebrate that. You did it. I couldn't be happier for you and this new journey you are on.

Thank you for allowing me to spend these last 8 weeks with you and I can't wait to see you and your beautiful family. Here is to you and your new future.

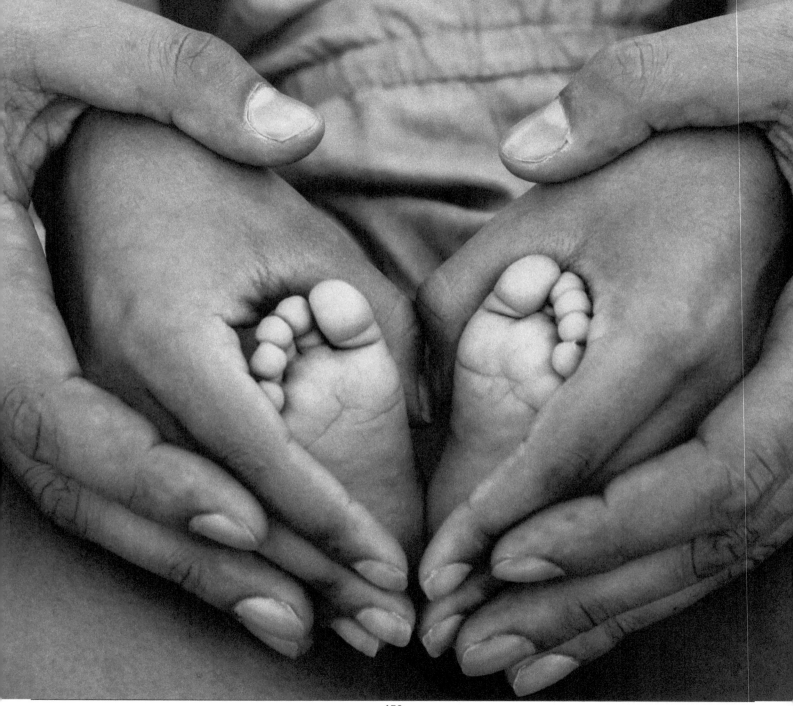

THANK YOU!

Follow us on...

Facebook
@kelahealthcoach

LinkedIn
@kelarobinsonsmith

and Instagram
@kela_healthcoach